COME INTO
OUR
WHIRL!

The First Cyber-Anthology of Poetry from the Poets Niche!

PLUS

The inspiring, never-before-revealed chronicle of chance meetings, actual email correspondence,and events which led to the creation of one of the fastest-growing, most unique, cyber-communities on the Internet!

Executive Editors: Monica Blache and Walt Goodridge

Published by a company called W

distributed worldwide by nichemarket.com

THE LEGAL STUFF

Books are available in bulk at discount prices. Single copies or available prepaid direct from the publisher.

Published by

a company called W
P.O. Box 618
Church Street Station
New York, NY 10008-0168

Marketed and Distributed on the world wide web by
nichemarket.com

Website: www.nichemarket.com
Emails: walt@nichemarket.com
              moni@nichemarket.com

DEDICATION

TO THOSE
NOT AFRAID TO
DREAM

ACKNOWLEDGMENTS

The Poets Niche thanks:

All of the featured poets who willingly consented to the use of their poetry in this anthology. Some of the poems in this anthology have been previously published and permission was granted by the authors to use their poems in COME INTO OUR WHIRL. The copyright of all poems are held by the individual authors of these poems.

We would like to thank Wilma Garnett, Cheryl Stocker and Jeanine Gautreaux, for their assistance and insightful opinions.

Many thanks to all the members of the Poets Niche for continuing to support us and seeing our vision.

Special thanks to Pamela Barnes, Rose Cooper, Afena Cobham, Rose Ford, Saleem Abdal-Khaaliq, Linval London, Tasha Tavaras, David Weeks, Tamshi Williams and Shenita Vanish, for volunteering their time, talents, and continued commitment to helping us make the dreams of many come true! Without their constructive opinions, enlightenment, and great sense of humor, the Poets Niche would not be a reality.

TABLE OF CONTENTS

Chapter One
>	moni's story	**11**
>	who the heck is moni?	**12**

Chapter Two
>	Walt's Introduction	**16**
>	How it all started	**21**
>	About the title	**22**

Chapter Three
>	YOU'VE GOT MAIL!	**23**

Chapter Four
>	Poetry by Poets Niche Members

Featured Poets:

Padmore Enyonam Agbemabiese
>	Africa	**70**
>	Our Prayers	**72**
>	Prophecy	**74**

/bams
>	in tender days {dear mama}	**75**
>	the all-purpose poem, generic aisle no.1	**76**
>	ghetto pets	**78**

Dorothy Benner
>	Don't	**80**
>	Loss of Innocence	**80**

Sandra Bushell
>	Wrinkle in Time	**82**
>	Speak to Me	**83**

Taheba Byrd
>	A New Look on Life	**86**
>	This is the Year	**86**

Angela Jones-Carr
>	Soul Searching	**88**
>	Love Complications	**89**

Shaun Cecil
      Rusty Knight   **91**
      Again **92**

Tina Marie Clark
      A Black Man   **93**
      Little Black Girl   **93**

Rodney Coates
      Old School Love   **95**
      Road of No Return   **98**

MOCHA (B. Afena Cobham)
      Blank Pages: A Black Woman's Voice   **99**
      PARTY LINE MADNESS: 1-800 BLACK GENOCIDE **100**
      Black Frame of Reference   **101**

Phaedra Davis
      Loveless and Fearless **102**
      My Game Has Changed **103**

Rene L. Davis
      Loving Me for Me   **105**
      Somebody tell me how **108**

Tracy Evans
      "God Bless The Child" (to L.O.M.)   **110**
      Untitled   **112**

Stephanie Griswold-Ezekoye
      The Troubled Heart   **113**
      Are you a little woman man   **114**

L. K. Rose Ford
      The woman that had you   **115**
      Lye Soap and "Conglomeration Soup" **116**

Craig Gill
      Untitled   **119**
      Untitled   **120**

Shawn Goins
>The Greeting **121**
>Adversary **122**

Christopher Hare
>The Beast Within **123**
>The Lonely Diva **124**

Susan Harrigan
>Mixed Emotions **125**
>Vision **126**

Nadeen Herring
>Son **128**
>Good Natured **129**

Akilah Holyfield
>The Eye Dance **130**
>Night **130**

Sharyn P. Hunter
>First **131**
>Descendants **131**

Saleem Abdal-Khaaliq
>Correction Fluid **132**
>The Sixth Generation Child **133**

Ghada El Kurd
>I remember **135**
>Reflecting 136

Ajani Kush
>White Heat **137**
>'bout time **138**
>Have Mercy (a sista's story) **139**

Jaci LaMon
>the breakup, chapter two **141**
>a woman's mood **142**
>three **143**

Dawn Landon
> Dreams of Bob **145**
> Reflecting on Love with Neff   **146**

Linval Hopeton London
> On this Morning (A Wedding Poem)   **148**
> Craving   **150**

Marilyn Marshall
> My Sweet King, I Am On My Throne   **151**
> Let me take the throne as your African Queen   **152**

Felicia Mason
> 360 Degrees   **154**
> Untitled   **155**

Nicole McLean
> Loneliness   **157**
> Damn...I'm almost 30!   **160**

Robin Porter
> No More Me   **163**
> A Rose   **163**

Karen Roberts
> The Box   **165**
> Ready   **167**

Angela Singletary
> revolution conversation piece   **168**
> are you in love with me   **169**

Sidney Singleton
> No Prayers Goes Unanswered   **171**
> Black Orchid   **172**

Demeterius Smith
> When Least Expected   **173**
> It Only Takes One Sip   **174**

Katherine Smith
> Colored   **177**
> Emancipated Again   **179**

Tasha Tavaras
    The Hush   **181**
    #L   **182**

David Weeks
    You Are My Black Woman   **183**
    Still Waters   **184**
    One Moment   **185**

Tamshi Williams
    Father Who   **187**
    Black By Nature; Proud By Choice   **187**
moni's poems
    Holding the Silence   **189**
    Held the Silence   **190**
    Ease   **191**
    5 Days Remembered   **194**

        ****

Chapter Five: There's Nothing Like Team Work
    Introduction   **196**

    Saleem Abdal-Khaaliq and Monica Blache
    S&M   **197**

    David Weeks and /bams
    duet (one groove)   **199**

    Padmore Agbemabiese and L. K. Rose Ford
    SO LONG THE ROAD   **201**

    James London and Taheba Byrd
    OUT TOO LATE   **202**

    GROUP POEM
    WHEN WHIRLS COLLIDE   **207**

Chapter Six: Features   **208**
    Features (moni's Top 10 & From the Queen's Throne)

AFTERWHIRL   **221**

Chapter One

MONI'S STORY

"COME INTO OUR WHIRL" is about dreams becoming reality. My journey is not unlike many of the featured poets. There are two principles of life that I believe in -- (1) nothing in life is coincidental or accidental; and (2) if you think or speak it, it becomes your reality.

That being said, after my son graduated from college in May 1998, I told my family and friends that it was time for me to claim my reward for the years I sacrificed putting him through college. My reward for a job well done was to meet new people who enjoyed the same things I enjoyed, and join a book club or a writer's group. Two weeks after thinking and speaking it, it became my reality.

It was through an unfortunate (or so I thought) glitch, bump in the road on the superhighway, or this thing called email, that my journey took a strange twist. In June 1998, I received Walt's Friday Inspiration #30. I read it, deleted it, and asked to be removed from his mailing list because I didn't know anyone named Walt. End of story? Not quite. Naturally, the following Friday I received another Walt's Friday Inspiration. Again, I read it, deleted it and requested to be removed from his mailing list. I think you know where I'm going with this -- obviously, I was not removed from Walt's mailing list. It was at that exact point in time which OUR WHIRLS collided.

Using the "If you build it, they will come" philosophy, the ripple from a single act created the Poets Niche. What started off as a small group of individuals is now a community of friends sharing their poetry with each other and receiving honest feedback and inspiration. Malidoma Patrice Som, from West Africa describes a community as, "Community doesn't mean that our family has to be there. . .We must look for people who value who we are, who see our gifts and whom we can then bring together as a form of community. . .We're talking about a community made up of people to whom you can really open up your heart without being hurt or rejected." Therefore, the Poets Niche is a supportive group of poets sharing their gifts with each other and now with you, in "COME INTO OUR WHIRL".

Being a part of this community of poets has changed me so profoundly, that my life will never be the same. I welcome you to sit for a spell, flip through the pages of our family album, and COME INTO OUR WHIRL.

OK, SO WHO THE HECK IS MONI?

Many of our members wondered, WHO'S MONI? Many only know me by my voice (which is a cross between professionalism and a little of don't play with me boy attitude), depending on the time of day you happen to talk to me. Before the truth is exposed in the tabloids, here's the unauthorized and un-unauthorized version of "WHO THE HECK IS MONI?"

moni and two of her son's works of art

UNAUTHORIZED VERSION

Where do I begin? I was born in the backseat of a van of gypsies, on the way to a carnival. OOPS! Is that my story or did I read that somewhere? I'm a single, 40 year old, freelance writer, living somewhere between Mardi Gras Lane and Gumbo Bayou. I'm also the proud mother a/k/a ATM machine, of a 21 year old artist, who is currently attending graduate school in New York.

UN-UNAUTHORIZED VERSION

Back to the beginning. There are three accomplices responsible for all the madness - my father, mother and high school English teacher.

Accomplice No. 1 - When I was in kindergarten, my teacher asked the class what did we want to be when we grew up? From the mind of a five year old, my first response was I wanted to be tall. (I'm only 5ft, which explains my answer even way back then). She smiled, then re-phrased the question. I thought for a second and said, "I want to be the President of the United States." (Little did I know I'd be accused of sleeping with the President, or was that Bill Hinton?) Anyway. . .

All the boys laughed and yelled, "Girls can't be the President." Boys were stupid anyway, and they certainly didn't know everything. I remembered hearing that it was an important job, but I really didn't know what the President did. Soooo, my quick come back was, "I mean, I want to be Mrs. President of the United States." (Go Hillary!!) This time, no one laughed.

However, that question bothered me all day. My first mistake was asking my dad what the President did. You see, my father was a history teacher. He pulled out this big book (which I later found out was an encyclopedia), and tried to explain the election process to a five year old. Two hours later, I decided to change my career. "Because I know how to write all my ABC's, I think I'll be a writer instead," I declared. My dad laughed and said, "You can be anything you want to be when you grow up, and daddy will buy it for you."

Accomplice No. 2 - My mother is probably most responsible for creating a monster. Whenever I disagreed with her rules or punishments (which was always), she allowed me to express my opinions, in what she called the "mad letters". Each "mad letter" had to meet certain criteria. I had to explain what I was angry about, whether I was right or wrong, and if I was her, list suggestions of how I would have handled the situation better. Back then, I was mad about everything -- going to bed before The Ed Sullivan Show, and especially the dreaded, early summertime curfew. The mad letter technique was an excellent teaching tool. It was through these written expressions of anger and resolution, I again declared I wanted to be a writer when I grew up.

Accomplice No. 3 - My high school English teacher is responsible for my stage fright. Every time I had to read or recite a poem (always standing in front of the class), one of two things happened -- I fainted, or I threw up. Needless to say, after throwing up for about a month, and my so-called friends complaining about vomit on their shoes, Ms. "P" came up with a plan. She ordered a podium. Well, it worked. First, the podium would break my fall. Second, any urge I had to vomit would be right there in my face. I still get a little queasy speaking in front of large groups. Now, I just warn people ahead of time not to sit in the front row.

Between my father buying my first typewriter when I was eight, my mother's mad letter exercises, and my English teacher putting a sign on the door "NO VOMITING ALLOWED," my future was inevitable.

As a teenager, I kept a diary that chronicled my thoughts, emotions, and dreams. This was the beginning of my so-called writing career. High school and college were testing grounds to display my talent. Lack of validation and negative influences altered my path. For the past 20 years, I have worked in the corporate arena expecting my skills and work ethics to be rewarded. However, through honest soul-searching, I discovered that self-worth comes from inner harmony. Therefore, the road I had taken simply brought me back to the beginning - my dream of becoming a writer.

Writing is my only form of creative expression. In September 1992, I co-authored and self-published my first book of poetry, The Mirror of Perception. Twelve local bookstores in New Orleans agreed to sell our book. I think we made enough to buy lunch that week. I've been told that poetry is not a very lucrative market. My belief, however, is any commercial success is lagniappe. But that's not why I write. I write because NO ONE CAN EXPRESS HOW I FEEL about my life experiences better than me. I also hope that my poems provide some comfort and communicate to those facing difficult times, that they are not alone. Whatever affects my sister or brother, whether it be disease, homelessness, injustice, pain or hope, it affects me.

I believe I've been called to the ministry of storytelling. Like the hieroglyphics our ancestors left behind, I too want to continue telling stories. Currently, I am working on my second and third books of poetry, and a suspense novel.

Just when I got accustomed to feeling sorry for myself about my career choice (keeping my day job to support my writing hobby), I received my first Walt's Friday Inspiration. And as they say, the rest is history!

That pretty much sums things up. The HBO version of WHO THE HECK IS MONI is under production. Whoopi has agreed to play MONI. (Just kidding. I intend to play myself).

moni

Moni is a freelance writer living in New Orleans, Louisiana. Her work has been published in Christian newsletters, anthologies, local and nationwide newsletters, magazines, and on numerous websites.

Chapter Two

WALT'S INTRODUCTION:

How to Understand, Experience, Appreciate, And Have Your Whirl Rocked by The Poets Niche!
by Poets Niche founder Walt Goodridge

Something unique!

This book is an attempt to share with you something that cannot be shared. It is something that can only be experienced firsthand and then remembered. There's a thrill of being in the moment that no words can ever capture, for it is the "thrill of nowness". Even I, as founder of the Poets Niche can never know what it is to be a member of the Poets Niche. For it is many things to many people. I can only watch in awe, and hope to glimpse its impact on others through the words that they share. If all this sounds a bit cryptic, it's only because, well, it's meant to be!

To really appreciate the Poets Niche, one first has to understand the uniqueness of what is happening in the world at this time. When the Internet was first conceived, it was intended as a way to share information and bring scientific minds together to tackle the problems of the world. It has, in part, accomplished much more than that in the everyday lives of average people. The Internet has created a new reality for all of us. In a very real sense, it has brought back the art of communication. People are learning all over again the power of language, the power of the written word. Communication is back in style!

Think about it, letter-writing is an art which was almost extinct until recently. And while we're likely to see LESS stamp licking in the future, and while penmanship suffers in this new digital age, "wordsmithing" is on the rise.

Thanks to the Internet, everyone is an author! So now you can think about what you want to say, compose it so that it's coherent to someone else, and by virtue of the "send" button on your browser, you can share these thoughts with others around the globe! Our human need to communicate in the most efficient way possible has gone from drums, smoke signals, runners, the pony express, morse code, surface mail, overnight delivery and now email!

"....Everyone's a star! We have some of the most unique individuals in the world in our little niche!"--**Walt Goodridge, Poets Niche Founder**

And for poets and writers especially, it's a much welcomed trend! Creative folk who yearn to be heard no long have to rely on live performances, radio, movies or television to be heard. The World Wide Web has made the ability to share words and ideas with others available to almost everyone! Websites and word of mouth (which I more accurately refer to as "word of email") by virtue of the "forward" button has made performers of us all!

Where would you go to meet people who shared your interests? People go to clubs, they attend concerts, they sign up for pottery courses, attend plays all with an underlying motive of meeting people like themselves. Our need to connect with others like us is a driving force in most of our lives. And we've had to make time to meet people, while holding down a job, keeping up with the payments, raising children, etc. Well, not anymore! Today we can do all this without disrupting the current flow of our lives. Despite the stresses of making a living in today's society, the internet has brought back the art of meeting people!

So thanks to the Internet revolution, you can communicate, create, meet, mingle and share with others on your wavelength all without ever leaving your cubicle at work, or your study at home.

Online communities like the Poets Niche are the wave of the present! They introduce a much-needed element of expression, fun and connectivity into our lives through the power of computers, laptops and wireless communication. And you can squeeze it in at work, at home, on the beach on a plane or while excercising in the gym, wherever!

Imagine if you will, a family, community, sharing, where the basic human need to affect others through language is encouraged and supported. The Internet offers many people an outlet of expression for aspects of their personalities which may otherwise remain dormant and hidden. People are bolder online. The inherent anonymity allows a freedom of expression which otherwise may go unnurtured in our society.

Welcome to the world of the Poets Niche!

The Power is in the unfolding

Scenario: Yesterday a friend emailed you about a website where you can join a group of poets and share your poetry. Having been a closet poet for the past few years, you decide to check it out and sign up to be part of something called the Poets Niche email discussion group. Within a few hours, you get welcome emails from people all over the country and a few overseas who welcome you to the group and express their excitement at getting to read some of your work!

"This is pretty cool", you think, and before you go to bed, you select one of your favorite poems to send to a single email address which automatically distributes your poem to your group of poets. You're a little nervous, but decide to give it a try!

You rise today having shared a poem yesterday, and in your mailbox are the supportive words of people you've never met, who say you've got talent and they'd like to read more! You're excited and can't wait to share some more!

Over the coming weeks, you develop friendships with people you never would have met otherwise, and find out it's a pretty ok group of people you've tapped into...

You share with one member that today is your birthday, and suddenly your inbox is flooded with well-wishers from people all over the world who seem genuinely happy you were born!

Perhaps you are a PhD candidate and a few days before graduation, you find that 100 people you know only by their email names, are congratulating you on your accomplishments.

Perhaps your pre-teenage daughter has been emotionally distant since her father passed away, and as a result of being part of the niche is now expressing a "form of happiness [you] hadn't seen in a very long time"

Maybe you're a child of divorce, and you check your email to find a poem that puts into words EXACTLY what you've been thinking about and experiencing all your life and never knew there were others who did too.

The group is now part of your life, and checking your email becomes a daily ritual which brings joy, excitement, new ideas, new people and an added chapter of your life that did not exist before!

And, trust me, I can tell you story upon story of how people's lives have been affected by this unique group of people, but the essence of it, the true power of the Poets Niche lies in the actual experience. The Poets Niche is nothing to you unless you are a part of it. It's like that old philosophy question, "If a tree falls in the forest and there's no one to hear it, does it make a sound?" Well, if something unique is growing in cyberspace but you're not there to experience it.....does it really exist? I believe that the Poets Niche is only truly real as a day by day unfolding for the people who are a part of it. There's a rhythm and flow that is unique to each moment in time. The interactions of this day capture a moment that will forever belong only to those who experienced it.

We do indeed have something quite unique in the Poets Niche. You won't find anything else like it anywhere. The unique collection of individuals, this moment in time will never be duplicated! It would have been something completely different than it is today, IF you had joined it. AND only you can affect what it will become simply be being a part of it now!

Our power is in the moment
and our life is in the now
we're all like actors in this drama
step right in and take a bow

and Our Whirl is but a chapter
of unique lives intertwining
and each story's a reflection
of this group whose star is shining

see it happen as we make it
know we're truly breaking ground
and from now till world eternal
another such will not be found

Our performances are captured
all our words are now the show
you and me each just as special
now in print for all to know

what new things have we created
to make your life now twice as rich
add us to your life and journey
....welcome to our Poets niche!

We're all stars!

In Come Into Our Whirl, you'll read the exciting origin story, meet a cast of performers that you'll come to know through their poetry, their emails, as well as what others say about them. You'll read "moni's Top 10" [what I call the soul of the Poets Niche] and live the week-to-week drama of it's unfolding. In this performance, however, there were no auditions, no screen tests, no membership cards, there are no bit parts, because everyone's a star! I'm very proud to be part of the cast of characters that have assembled here. But know beyond all doubt, that we don't really exist unless and until YOUR life is part of the story. So, I invite you not only to be a spectator of the show that has transpired thus far, but a participant in the drama that is about to unfold. We await your voice!

The Poets Niche
the creation of one
the soul of another
the voice of many
the life of us all

HOW IT ALL STARTED

"The Poets Niche was a spinoff of Walt's Friday Inspirations!"

FOR IMMEDIATE RELEASE

Silver Spring, MD: Every week, in homes and offices around the world, thousands of people tune in regularly to what has become a popular Internet tradition: a show of sorts by Walt Goodridge, former Civil Engineer, now turned entrepreneur and e-performer. Walt, now known throughout cyberspace as "The Inspirer" motivates tens of thousands every Friday with each "episode" of a unique journey he calls *Walt's Friday Inspirations*. Now in it's second year, the Inspirations are achieving cultlike status among it's followers, and now has a website, spawned a Poets Niche, an advice column called "Ask the Inspirer", a fanclub, and has led to his new book entitled *Lessons In Success from the Silent Performer* (the first of a planned 4 part quest). And it all started with a single email!

"It's amazing how this has grown!" says Walt. The list started with a few of my close friends and business partners, and now includes over 26,000 people all over the world! Now I get hundreds of emails each week from people who share with me how the Inspirations are helping them at the job, at home, in relationships, and simply in understanding life. It's a great feeling to know that something like this is having a real impact."

So why does he do it? A firm believer of success through personal growth, Walt believes that thoughts create reality. "Success is about having the right thoughts and then consistently thinking and acting on them to bring you closer to your dreams. Unfortunately most of us don't get enough practice weilding the type of thoughts that can cut through the weeds and traps we've thought ourselves into". It was with this goal in mind that he started first quoting and then composing his own "thoughts that create success" which now not only inspire others, but tell a story and provide a peek into his own private journey of discovery. Walt's mission statement: "I share what I know so that others may grow!"

ABOUT THE TITLE

Like the press release says, people started getting into what I was doing with the Inspirations. As each week went by, I offered more of my thoughts in verse and rhyme. One of my favorite Inspirations (#46), gives an inside peek into what was happening at the time as the Poets Niche started to grow...

In a lake quite still
I dipped my hand
and stirred to make it spin
The motion touched a kindred soul
and someone else joined in

caught in the swirl and pulled inside
like driftwood by the sea
a thousand hearts and minds joined in
attracted by my dream

like wisps of breeze that father storms
and shake the world with force
my little spiral fully grown
pulls mighty ships off course

this movement
now on its own (r)evolves
and draws whole nations in
the ripple from a single act
that caused the world to spin

The Poets Niche was born....but let's not jump ahead of ourselves. As I said, it all started with a single email......

Chapter Three

"YOU'VE GOT MAIL!"

Date: Friday, June 12, 1998
From: buttaphly2000@hotmail.com (love eternal)
To: walt@nichemarket.com
Subject: Suggestions

Dear Walt,

     First let me thank you for adding me to your list! I love your Friday inspirations, all of your poems are beautiful. Which brings me to my suggestion: I also think that you should have a poet's niche. I am an aspiring Poet myself and I think that your site is a great way for myself and other young poets to get exposure for our work. I love communicating with other poets and bouncing ideas off of people who love poetry just like I do.

     Thanks for listening,

```
/~~~~~~~~~~~~~~~~~~~~~~~~~~~~~~~~~~~~~~~~~~~~~~~~~~~~~~~~\
```
Date: 98-05-29 08:19:30 EDT

To: Walt@nichemarket.com

From: Mocha

Hi Walt, I'm considering staying on your listserv, however, I do have a question.
Does this website offer a Poetry section for upcoming Poets?

let me know,
Mocha

```
/~~~~~~~~~~~~~~~~~~~~~~~~~~~~~~~~~~~~~~~~~~~~~~~~~~~~~~~~\
```
Date: Saturday, May 30, 1998

To: Mocha

From: Walt@nichemarket.com

Subject: Your poetry

Mocha:

A Poets Niche would be cool. Quite a few people have requested it.

Let's keep in touch on that one...and if you have any poetry to share, please feel
free.

Walt

```
/~~~~~~~~~~~~~~~~~~~~~~~~~~~~~~~~~~~~~~~~~~~~~~~~~~~~~~~~\
```
Date: Friday, June 12, 1998

To: walt@nichemarket.com

From: MHCWoman@aol.com

Subject: A personal thanks from Walt plus....

Greetings!!

Poets Niche would be wonderful. Here is a link to a site where my poetry is
being featured...for inspiration sake! Please enjoy!

jaci

```
/~~~~~~~~~~~~~~~~~~~~~~~~~~~~~~~~~~~~~~~~~~~~~~~~~~~~~~~~~~~\
```

Date: Tuesday, June 16, 1998
To: moni
From: walt@nichemarket.com
Subject: Help with the Poets Niche!

Hi Moni:

Thanks for the support! Let's talk.

I'm definitely excited about a possible collaboration! We can correspond a bit, or
talk on the phone about some ideas to see if we are on the same wavelength!

Meanwhile, tell me a bit more about yourself. (location, business interests,
projects, goals, dreams, etc!)

Walt

```
/~~~~~~~~~~~~~~~~~~~~~~~~~~~~~~~~~~~~~~~~~~~~~~~~~~~~~~~~~~~\
```

Date: Tuesday, June 16, 1998
To: Walt@nichemarket.com
From: moni
Subject: Help with the Poets Niche!

Walt:

Call me in the a.m. around 8:15CST - XXX/XXX-XXXX

moni

So I called moni the next day
and we talked for awhile and
hit it off! Turns out she's in
New Orleans, Louisiana.

```
/~~~~~~~~~~~~~~~~~~~~~~~~~~~~~~~~~~~~~~~~~~~~~~~~~~~~~~~~\
```

Date: Friday, June 19, 1998
To: Walt@nichemarket.com
From: Tasha
Subject: Poetry

To whom it may concern:

I would like to be involved in the creation of the Poets Niche. Please e-mail me
more info on how I can be a part of this project.

Peace & Blessings
Tasha "Blakbutterfly" Tavaras

THIS IS THE ORIGINAL EMAIL SENT LAUNCHING THE POETS NICHE, WHICH WAS SENT TO 15 OF THE ORIGINAL

CHARTER MEMBERS.

```
/~~~~~~~~~~~~~~~~~~~~~~~~~~~~~~~~~~~~~~~~~~~~~~~~~~~~~~~~\
```

Date: Sunday, June 21, 1998
To: All Poets
From: Walt@nichemarket.com
Subject: Hi from Walt re: Poets Niche

Hi:

I'm sending this out to everyone who has responded positively in favor/request of
a Poets Niche on the Niche Market Exclusives Site.

Good news: We're on our way, and it will be because of you!

Once I'm able to connect with my server account (is it just me or is the internet a
bit slow recently?) I'll be setting up a Poets Niche discussion group where we'll
be able to have a brainstorming session to set goals and get under way, and
where all the members will be able to meet and greet each other!

Thanks and stay tuned! Big things are on the way!

Walt
P.S. (If you don't wish to be a part of the discussion group, please let me know
now)

To: All Poets
From: Walt@nichemarket.com
Subject: The Poets Niche is officially on!!! Please reply

Dear Poets Niche "Member":

This is Walt. Thanks for responding to my email.
 I've set up a Poets Niche discussion group distribution list at
poets@nichemarket.com which includes everyone who responded to my request,
or who has shown an interest in a Poets Niche by email or otherwise.

Here's how it works: As a member of the group, whenever you send your
thoughts, ideas, questions, responses, etc. to (poets@nichemarket.com), every-
one in the group will get a copy of your email and have the chance to respond to
you. Please send responses also to (poets@nichemarket.com). So that way we'll
all be involved in the discussion.

Once things get going, you'll want to check your email at least once a day, so we
can move forward quickly.

Any questions?

I'd like to kick off the brainstorming session for the Poets Niche with the follow-
ing question:

1. What should be our goal for the Poets Niche? Please respond with an intro-
duction (unless you want to remain anonymous).

Walt

Date: Tuesday, June 23, 1998 6:04 AM
To: Poets@nichemarket.com
From: walt@nichemarket.com
Subject: Suggestions for Poets Niche

*NOTE: It seems a few people on the list didn't receive the email launching the
Poets Niche, so I'll resend it to all. Also, remember to send your responses to
(poets@nichemarket.com). That way, everyone on the list will get a copy of
your email and be able to respond.

Q: What should be our goal for the Poets Niche? Should we also provide a way for poets to sell their work? Please respond with an introduction (unless you want to remain anonymous).

This is my introduction:

The goal of the Poets Niche is to insight, provoke and entertain, through the muse of the thoughts which flow through one's mind at a given moment of time, whether that be a positive or negative nature...expression...the ultimate expression...

Please respond ASAP!!

Walt

/~~~~~~\

Date:	Tuesday, June 23, 1998
To:	Poets@nichemarket.com
From:	moni
Subject:	Suggestions for Poets Niche

GOOD MORNING FELLOW MEMBERS!!! I also like the introduction. I am a true believer in "what you believe and what you put out," will certainly come back to you. We are only being tested by the obstacles we put in our own way. Love, generosity, compromise, humility, etc., are all tools God has given us to make this a better world. It's up to us how we use these tools to make this a better place. With that being said, I hope the use of profanity or pornography will not be published under this website.

I look forward to working with each and everyone of you, as well as reading your poetry.

HAVE A GREAT DAY!!!

Monica a/k/a moni

/~~~~~~\

Date:	Tuesday, June 23, 1998
To:	Poets@nichemarket.com
From:	walt@nichemarket.com
Subject:	Suggestions

I personally like "P's" suggestion that writers/poets/poetesses should get paid for their works. It's in line with my beliefs that when you do what you love, the money will follow. I believe that's in synch with the way the universe works that when you find your talent and contribute to others enjoyment and well being (just the same as a doctor or performer) that the world is enriched by your giving and you should expect to be enriched in return. It's the eternal flow of give and receive that on which the universe is based. Of course, these are MY views and I've made a decision that I'll go with whatever the majority of the Poets Niche feel this group should be committed to.

By the way, feel free to spread the word about what we've got here. I'm sure you guys know of others who might be interested in joining up. Just tell them to email me to put them on the Poets Niche group list. There'll be a form on the site in a few days.

Walt

/~~~~~~\

Date:	Tuesday, June 23, 1998
To:	Poets@nichemarket.com
From:	love eternal
Subject:	Suggestions for Poets Niche

I believe that our goal should be to receive feedback on our work from our peers. As poets and lovers of poetry, it is very important that we are able to talk honestly about our work. I also believe that we should try to give each other as much support as possible.

Peace & Blessings
Blakbutterfly

/~~~~~~\

Date:	Wednesday, June 24, 1998
To:	Poets@nichemarket.com
From:	XXXXX@aol.com
Subject:	Suggestions

I believe the primary goal should be to herd all of our creative thoughts, ideas, and musing together and eventually make up some kind of booklet or newsletter. It could be sent out to others who may not do any writings, but are interested in reading the creations of our fellow members. I would not mind submitting a poem or short story and I am positive that others feel the same way.
Thank you.

```
/~~~~~~~~~~~~~~~~~~~~~~~~~~~~~~~~~~~~~~~~~~~~~~~~~~~~~~~~~~~~~\
```

Date: Thursday, June 25, 1998
To: Poets@nichemarket.com
From: walt@nichemarket.com
Subject: Ok then ....

There are still some people who haven't pitched in a thought about our direction
(apparently, not all of us check our email hourly!). But, no matter, give me a day
or three to equip the site with something that will allow us to post our work and/
or to provide an archive of these email discussions.

Also I suggest we keep each other informed of events, sites and other goodies
which would be of interest and value to the promising, prospective published
poet!

Walt


```
/~~~~~~~~~~~~~~~~~~~~~~~~~~~~~~~~~~~~~~~~~~~~~~~~~~~~~~~~~~~~~\
```

Date: Sunday, June 28, 1998
To: Poets
From: Walt@nichemarket.com
Subject: So let's get going!

Hi all!

I'd like to start sharing poetry this week.

I think we should use the email list for information, advice, current events etc.,
and such. Therefore, email me directly at (Nichemrket@aol.com) with one poem
which you would like highlighted on the website. I'm also considering creating a
(weeklypoem@nichemarket.com) autoresponder. Where you can send an email
to (weeklypoem@nichemarket.com) and you get the
Poem of the Week automatically sent back to you. (Feedback please).

I'll choose a few to highlight every few days!

P.S. - Please keep it as short as possible. (This because of the public's attention
span. Don't hate me, I just tell it like it is!)

Walt

One of the first poems we received was "Jonesin'" by Tasha and one of my personal favorites. [You'll have to visit the site to check it out!--Walt]

/~~~~~~\

Date:	Monday, June 29, 1998
To:	Walt@nichemarket.com
From:	Tasha
Subject:	"Jonesin'"

If it's too long (or too lame:) let me know! I think your suggestion of a "Poem of the Week" is great. I also think that we should be able to use the email list to give each other feedback on any of the work posted on the site. Let me know what you think. Thanks Walt!

Tasha

/~~~~~~\

Date:	Monday, June 29, 1998
To:	Tasha
From:	Walt
Subject:	"Jonesin'"

Hey I like that!

No, your poem is not long or lame, but it inspires, excites and delivers. One can just guess what the two lovers want and just thinking of it too makes me quiver.

Walt

~~~~~~

Needless to say, by this time I was getting excited about the possibilities of what we had on our hands. I also knew that if this were to grow, it would need the constant attention of people other than myself.

/~~~~~~\

Date:	Thursday, July 9, 1998 12:49 PM
To:	moni; buttaphly
From:	walt@nichemarket.com
Subject:	By the way!

Hi Ladies (and if the two of you haven't met, let me introduce you!)

From how vocal you've both been (thanks), I've identified the two of you as the core leaders of our movement. There might be one or two more you'll meet soon.

Our mission, should you decide to accept, is to make this the biggest website on the Internet!! As we proceed, I'll share with you letters and stuff I get so that you can understand why I'm excited!

I wanted to keep you up-to-date with what's going on since from my vantage point, there's more to see. Things are going great! Everyday more people are joining. Right now we have 32 members in the Poets Niche. (Would you guys want to be informed each time a new person joins?).

Without going into too much technical detail, I'm going to set things up on the site such that people can sign themselves up rather than me having to manually add people to the list.

We really have something good here. For right now, we're building a sense of excitement and community. My interest is to really find a way for it to be profitable for other poets and writers (am I being too materialistic?)

Anyway, write back and I'm going to start promoting big for Friday Inspiration #30. Any ideas you might want to add are welcomed!!

Walt

/~~~~~~\

Date: Tuesday, July 14, 1998
To: Tamshi
From: Tasha
Subject: I'll try to explain

Tam:

I'll try to explain this to the best of my ability! Let's say you have a poem you want to share with the group. You would send your poem to poets@nichemarket.com and everybody who is a part of the Poets Niche will receive a copy of your poem. Members usually respond quickly and feedback is positive. Periodically, you can check the website to see if one of your poems was voted Poem of the Week!!! That's basically it!! I hope I helped you out a bit!!

Once again, WELCOME!! We are happy you joined!!
Peace & BlessingsTasha

/~~~~~~\

Date: Tuesday, July 14, 1998
To: Poets Niche
From: moni
Subject: My poem

Dearest Fellow Members:

Monica here, from down south in New Orleans (NAWLINS), Louisiana. Below is my poem "The Wedding Night," for your review and/or comments.

Remember, nothing in life is accidental or coincidental. So, if you are HERE, VIA EMAIL) and communicating with us at this point in time, this was meant to be.

Continue writing and emailing your wonderful and thought provoking poems so we can ALL enjoy.

KEEPING THE LIGHT ON TO HELP YOU FIND YOUR WAY!!!
moni

```
/~~~~~~~~~~~~~~~~~~~~~~~~~~~~~~~~~~~~~~~~~~~~~~~~~~~~~~~~\
```

Date: Wednesday, July 15, 1998
To: Poets@nichemarket.com
From: Walt
Subject: A secret about Buttaphly

>psst>

Hey everyone! I'm not one to talk, so you didn't hear this from me...but word on
the street is that today is Buttaphly's Birthday!!!

For those of you who haven't had a chance to meet her...Poets Niche member and
universal conduit supreme, Tasha T, was one of the driving forces behind the
development of the Poets Niche. It was her email, along with a few others, that
joined the swirl that shakes the world!

[insert shameless self-promotion here:] (but of course, you'll be able to read all
about that in a upcoming book.

.... but I'm not one to gossip...
Walt

```
/~~~~~~~~~~~~~~~~~~~~~~~~~~~~~~~~~~~~~~~~~~~~~~~~~~~~~~~~\
```

Date: Wednesday, July 15, 1998
To: Tasha
From: moni
Subject: You are too Sweet!!!

Girl!!

You are too much *lol*. I thank you for your sweet words!!! I loved the
poem!!! What did I do to deserve all this Love??? Anyway, thank you again!!

Peace & much love
Tasha

```
/~~~~~~~~~~~~~~~~~~~~~~~~~~~~~~~~~~~~~~~~~~~~~~~~~~~~~~~~\
```

Date: Wednesday, July 15, 1998
To: moni
From: XXXXX
Subject: Your poem

A friend of mine is getting married & needs a poem..........could I suggest that she
use yours? (w/ credit and acknowledgments made).

/~~~~~~\

Date: Sunday, July 19, 1998
To: Poets@nichemarket.com
From: love eternal
Subject: Thanks & Welcome

What's up!!!

THANKS everybody for your kind words and thoughts on my birthday. I am so
thankful for all of this love. I would have responded sooner, but with all the
events of the National Black Arts Festival, I was trying to vibe as much as
possible!!!

I want to extend a very warm welcome to all of the newest members of our
family!!! I hope that you will share as much of your work as you feel comfort-
able!! I would also like to say Congratulations to everybody who was selected
for Poems of the Week!!

Peace & Blessings
Tasha

/~~~~~~\

Date: Thursday, July 23, 1998
To: Poets@nichemarket.com
From: Mocha
Subject: I wanted to share . . .

First, I apologize to those who want to be removed from the list, but if it hasn't
happened yet, I don't mean to send you more email than you need.

HOWEVER, it's just been confirmed that I am a XXXXX Powerball winner!!!
hahahaha. I got five numbers and of course I'm playing again. Ya might be in
the company of a future Millionaire *smile*!!!
Peace
Mocha

Date: Friday, July 24, 1998
To: Mocha
From: Moni
Subject: I wanted to share . . .

Mocha:
GirRRRRllll. Good news travels fast. Long time no see. I'm yo twin brother's
cousin, on yo daddy's side, next to yo other auntie's grandma's uncle, side of the
family. Girl, you might not believe this, but I was just praying to God, I said,
"Lawd, I sho needs me XXXX dollars!" And here you go and wins my money!!!
Well, you think you can break me off a lil somethin', cause I gots to get my hair
done today so I can go out with Jethro tonight. He likes it when I gets my hair
did!!!

Girl, congrats. Enjoy this because you deserve it. Use it to get your book
published. Have a great weekend!!

yo sis
moni

Date: Friday, July 24, 1998
To: Nichemrket@aol.com; poets@nichemarket.com
From: David

Greetings & Good Mawnin' EveryOne!

I want 2 thank everyone for their positive responses 2 my poems, I am honored.
Here is the other part 2 my companion piece that I sent yesterday...Brothers, this
one is for Us...enjoy!!

David
"Ancient"

Date: Tuesday, July 28, 1998
To: Poets@nichemarket.com
From: Tamshi
Subject: Welcome

I just want to welcome all of the new brothas and sistas to the Niche and hope
you will begin sharing your poems with us real soon.
Tam

/~~~~~~\

Date:	Thursday, July 30, 1998
To:	moni
From:	ROSEFORMS
Subject:	My signature poem

Dearest Rose!!!!

Honey chile, "The Woman That Had You" just pulled me right in. This was the line I read when the floodgates opened: "She was surprised, with a tear in her eye, when you thanked everybody, but her you passed by." I cried like a baby!!!!

Where do I find, "life ain't nothing but a series of words" Book II? I just love, love, love this title.

Honey, ROSEEEEE, girl. Need I say more!!!!!

peace
moni

/~~~~~~\

Date:	Thursday, July 30, 1998
To:	moni
From:	walt@nichemarket.com
Subject:	Ideas for the Poets Niche

Here's what I'd like to see happen!! Brainstorm of ideas!!

- Goal: To create the most popular site on the internet!
- Goal: To be interviewed on Oprah
- Goal: To be featured on AOL live!
- Launch a "Poets Niche Series" of Books
- Because of the support among the members of the Poets Niche, our books debut at number one   on the Bestseller's List!
- Poets get income from sale of books featuring their poetry
- We can also publish novels and short stories
- Need a new logo for the site (I'll work on that one)
- What other things can we do to get people to keep coming back to the site?
- Who do we know to contact to generate publicity for what's going on?

Walt

/~~~~~~\

Date: Friday, July 31, 1998
To: Moni Blache
From: Walt Goodridge, Executive Director
Subject: Position: Really nice person who help people in the Poets Niche

Hi moni!

Congratulations on your new position and welcome to Nichemarket.com! You
are now officially authorized to represent yourself as "The Really Nice Person
Who Helps People in the Poets Niche" on behalf of Nichemarket.com.

STATS:
- Approximately 20,000 people are on the Nichemarket.com main list
- As of today, there are 64 members in the Poets Niche

Immediate GOALS:
1. Come up with Mission Statement (we can do this together)
2. Get membership up

Long Term Goals: (like within 6 months!)
1. To make this a profitable venture (sell ads, market books, etc.)
2. To assist in making Nichemarket.com the most popular and visited site on the
internet.

How: Word of mouth campaign is the best way to do this. Brainstorm on con-
tent, features, services and other unique stuff we can offer.

TASKS:
You'll no doubt come up with your own tasks on how to get this done!

Ready? Let's have fun with this!

Walt

/~~~~~~\

Date: Thursday, August 6, 1998
To: James London
From: moni
Subject: New stuff

James:

I know the secret of why you are such a beautiful soul. He filled your emptiness. He opened the doors. He touched your heart. And, He's living within you. We are the lucky ones to have crossed your path at a time when spirits need to be lifted. Your poems inspire us to live in unity and share the gift of love.

always
moni

Date: Thursday, August 6, 1998
To: Poets@nichemarket.com
From: walt@nichemarket.com
Subject: IMPORTANT: It's coming soon!

Hey all!

I'm fortunate enough to be getting some help from one of our poets, moni, with keeping the Poems of the Week running smoothly.

Rest assured, therefore, that she's working tirelessly on compiling the wonderful work all of you have been submitting and you'll start to see more of your work on the site within the next few days!

Walt

P.S. I wanted to reward her by bestowing upon her a title worthy of her greatness, but since she detests titles, we decided to go with TRNPATPNWKTRS which stands for "The Really Nice Person At The Poets Niche Who Keeps Things Running Smoothly".

/~~~~~~\

Date:	Sunday, August 9, 1998
To:	Poets@nichemarket.com
From:	Nichemrket@aol.com
Subject:	NEW! The Poets Niche Bulletin Board

Hi Poets:

I'm announcing the official launch of the Poets Niche Bulletin Board. Feel free to post information on events, gatherings, websites and anything of interest to poets. NO POEMS PLEASE. Send poems to the group at poets@nichemarket.com for us to use in the Poems of the Week site!

Walt

I'm constantly reminded of how perfectly lucky the Poets Niche was to have attracted moni. One of the first things she and I talked about, and which she put together was the Poets Niche Mission and Vision statement. Here it is in it's original form.

/~~~~~~\

Date:	Sunday, August 9, 1998
To:	Walt
From:	moni
Subject:	Mission Statement

Attached is the Draft Mission Statement!!!

POETS NICHE MISSION AND VISION STATEMENT

Our Motto: The vision of one can fulfill the dreams of many.

Our Mission

The Poets Niche is an online service created to provide poets a network base to showcase their poetry. We believe poetry tells the story of the poet. Like the hieroglyphics our ancestors left behind telling their stories, we want to help each member personally tell their story. Therefore, our goal is to empower our members with the knowledge, resources and expertise to globally market their poetry.

The Poets Niche and NicheMarket.com can and will become the most popular website on the Internet. How do we accomplish this goal? Most importantly it requires your help. Networking within your communities, advertising the Poets Niche in the media, radio, newspapers, talk shows, magazines, local writer's groups, universities, bookstores, coffee shops, places of employment! Word of mouth is how every great movement gets it's start and sustains its momentum. (And with the power of email, we can indeed create something the likes of which this world has never seen!)

On our end, we need to make sure we give you what you want and need to help you achieve your own goals, personal and otherwise. Let us know what you'd like to see the Poets Niche become, and I promise you, if enough people want it, we will make it happen!

Immediate Plans

1) Poems of the Week: Every week we will spotlight new Poets Niche members and their poems.

We believe that all poems posted on this website should inspire, uplift, motivate and be spiritual. Therefore, the use of profanity, pornography and the degrada-tion of any race or gender, will not
be posted on this website. We believe, however, in the freedom of expression, and ask that members continue to send their poems directly to the group. This will allow each poet to continue to receive comments and/or opinions about their poems from the members.

2) Bulletin Board - Poets Niche members who want to share and/or invite others to any upcoming events, either locally or nationally, should post these events on our Bulletin Board.

3) Poets Niche Who's Who - Our Who's Who puts a face with the poets and their poems. A photograph of the poet, and a short bio of each member will be posted on this website. (photos optional;we'll make an announcement when we're ready to start accepting pictures)

4) Poets Niche Book Profile - This website will profile the work of any member who has published a book(s) of poetry. This will allow the poet to market and sell their book(s) online.

Future Plans

1) Poets Niche Audio Room - Each member can personally read their poem(s) along with a little history about the poem on this page. Visitors to the site will be able to hear the recording of you performing your poetry!

2) Poets Niche Chat Room - We'll be having monthly board meetings, or just friendly chat sessions to meet, greet or discuss how to improve the Poets Niche, etc.

3) Writer's Resource Room - We will provide website resources and/or information on copyrighting, marketing, literary agents, etc.

4) Quarterly Contests - We will continue to have contests which will allow members to have their work exposed to the greatest number of people around the world!

5) Poets Niche Publishing/Poets Niche Anthologies - In the not so distant future, we will publish a series of Poets Niche Anthologies, which will include the top 50 poems of the year.

The Poets Niche would like to personally thank those members who have volunteered their time and efforts in making this website a reality.

Moni Blache--The Really Nice Person at the Poets Niche Who Keeps Things Running Smoothly
AND
Walt Goodridge--President NicheMarket.com

/~~~~~~\

Date: Sunday, August 9, 1998
To: moni
From: Walt
Subject: Not quite what I had in mind (Mission Statement)

IT'S A MILLION TIMES BETTER!!!!!!!

BUTTER!
THE BOMB!!!!
PHAT!!
SUPERB!
JOLLY GOOD!
QUITE IMPRESSIVE!
cool!

This will definitely be added to the Poets Niche website!!!

/~~~~~~\

Date: Tuesday, August 11, 1998
To: poets@nichemarket.com
From: walt@nichemarket.com
Subject: Things are moving ahead

Hi all:

Great news! We've just updated the Poems of the Week Section of the Niche!

New poems have been posted and an archive has finally been established. I'll be
releasing the official Mission Statement of the Poets Niche within the next 24
hours and would love some feedback from you about both these new develop-
ments.

I'll be setting up a real time chat/meeting (using AOL's Instant messenger--if you
need it, let me know) for later in the month. All are welcome to attend. We'll
meet and greet and discuss the future of the Niche. Until then....remember....

.success is a journey
not a destination!

Walt

Everyone who has joined the Poets Niche is a unique, talented, and special person. I've had a chance to speak directly with some, email others and simply read the poetry of others still. However, when" Padmore" joined the group, something quite unique happened. For me it was a defining moment of the early life of the Poets Niche. I read his work and was touched in quite a special way. I've since come to learn more about who Padmore Agbemabiese is, and feel quite honored that he is a part of our family.

Here's a correspondence from moni to Padmore which sort of echos the same sentiment...

/~~~~~~\

Date: Wednesday, August 19, 1998
To: Padmore
From: moni
Subject: PROPHECY

Padmore:

Welcome to the Poets Niche. I apologize for not responding and welcoming you sooner, but you know the standard reason -- work, work, and mo' work. Where are you writing us from?

Words can't express how much I am really, really, really enjoying your poems. Honey, you are toooo baaaadddddd, and downright touched with a precious GIFT -- i.e., capturing the soul and spirit of the reader with thought provoking words. I can't wait to read more.

Have you had a chance to view Poets Niche Mission Statement? And, if so, is there anything special you would like us at the Poets Niche to do or you would like to see?

Wishing you continued peace and blessings,

moni

Date:	Thursday, August 20, 1998
To:	moni
From:	Padmore
Subject:	PROPHECY

Thanks so much Monica. I am a Ghanaian. I came over to the US in 1997. I am graduating on September 3, 1998 with a Masters in African-American Literature. I have also been accepted into the Ph.D. [English] program at Ohio State University this Fall, 1998.

It is my hope to get a few poems of mine across to fellow poets and lovers of poetry. I want to get these poems published either in JOURNALS first or straight into a book. I love poetry and drama. My experience has set a beehive aflame in my mind. I plan to visit Ghana next summer to set up a communication network that sells the ideas of NICHEMARKET. I want to set up a Communication Center equipped with an African-American and African Studies Library [public] and a small Desktop Publishing network for creative writers. This is my goal in life and as I now join the NICHEMARKET, I hope you will sustain the interest and assist me in marketing the ideals of my mission. I hope to hear from you soon. Thanks.

Padmore

/~~~~~~\

Date:	Saturday, August 22, 1998
To:	Poets@nichemarket.com
From:	Nichemrket@aol.com
Subject:	Special thanks to everyone from Walt!!!

Hi all:

Just wanted to let you know how special all of you are! I'm having a great time meeting and chatting with many of you! I'm glad I listened to those suggestions WAY back then (it's only been two months, you know) to start the Poets Niche! Special thanks to Moni, thanks Buttaphly, thanks Jaci, thanks Mocha! Love you all!

We're all part of something really great and getting better!

Walt

A MAJOR ANNOUNCEMENT:

"We don't die, we multiply!"

Just two months after we started the Poets Niche, something quite interesting started to happen. We started to notice that people were leaving the group! At first I thought that perhaps these people were offended in some way by the poetry, or, perhaps, I thought, this wasn't going to be the long, ongoing ride moni and I envisioned.

Turns out that with close to 100 people in the group sharing poetry every day, people's email boxes were being filled with 20, 30 or so emails every day! It was getting overwhelming.

We convened and emergency meeting of the Executive Board (that's me and moni, in case you weren't paying attention) and threw around a couple of solutions and alternatives and decided that we would "split" the Poets Niche into two groups to cut down on the number of emails.

(The reference to "Bebe's Kids" in the email I sent comes from the Robin Harris animated movie of the same name. In it, Robin Harris' love interest, Bebe, seems to have more and more kids each time he visits her. The bratty, gun-toting offspring who tell Robin, "we don't die, we multiply!")

/~~~~~~\

Date: Monday, August 31, 1998
To: Poets@nichemarket.com
From: walt@nichemarket.com
Subject: from Walt: IMPORTANT ANNOUNCEMENT re: BEBE'S KIDS!!

Dear Poets!

There are 2 MAJOR ANNOUNCEMENTS which are being sent in 2 separate emails.

1. Expanding the Poets Niche! (effective Friday, September 4th)
2. (another email will follow soon re: Publishing The Poets Niche Anthology!)

1. SPLITTING THE POETS NICHE!

As you already know, the Poets Niche is growing! To deal with the ever increasing amounts of email that our members are getting, we are now ready to move into Phase II of what I call "The Rise of the Poets".

- We are going to be expanding the Poets Niche into 3 groups!
- Group 1 will share their work by sending poems to poets1@nichemarket.com
- Group 2 will send work to poets2@nichemarket.com and Poets3@nichemarket.com and so on. - You will be notified by email which group you fall into. Our goal here is to reduce the amount of email to individual members, while still retaining the community and family spirit that has developed in the Poets Niche.

HERE ARE SOME DETAILS TO MAKE IT ALL WORK SMOOTHLY:
-Each group will have from 20 to 30 members.
-Think of it--if you remember high school biology class--as an ameba splitting up into two identical versions of itself, then 4 then 8.....or better still as a fertilized egg splitting and multiplying..(Same baby, more parts to it.) Or just think of it as Bebe's Kids (we don't die, we just multiply!!) >ahem< just got a bit carried away there...
-If you fall into a group list and there's a particular person whose poetry you wish to receive who's not in your group, then contact that person and have them put you on their "CC" list.
-All groups will still be notified when a new person joins, that way we can all still greet them and make friends.
-Those of us who've been a part of the original group now for the past few months, it's up to us to keep the flavor of each new group consistent. The name of the game is mutual support, love and friendship! Let's take this thing to the next level!!!

Contact me at (walt@nichemarket.com) or moni@nichemarket.com with any questions.

Walt

Well, quite an interesting thing happened then! It seems quite a few of our poets, many of the original members, couldn't stand to miss out on some poems while receiving others. Could you imagine being in the Poets Niche, for example, and NOT being in the group that had Padmore in it!? I shudder to think!

/~~~~~~\

Date:	Friday, September 4, 1998
To:	Walt
From:	Craig G
Subject:	Expansion

Walt:

I have a question for you. I am currently a member of the Poets Niche and I was wondering, when the Poets Niche splits, can I be placed on all distribution lists? I don't have a problem receiving all of the emails. The Poets Niche is a great idea, keep up the good work.

Craig G

/~~~~~~\

Date:	Saturday, September 5, 1998
To:	moni@nichemarket.com
From:	Tamshi
Subject:	Put me on both lists

Hello Moni-Mon!

I want the full effect of the Poets Niche, so sign me up for both lists so I can read all the poems from our members. You are doing a wonderful job. Will talk to ya later~~~

Tam

/~~~~~~\

Date: Monday, September 7, 1998
To: Angela
From: moni
Subject: W E L C O M E

Dearest Angela:

Angela - Just read both your poems submitted on 8/27 & 8/31. 8/27 - LOVED
IT!!! Especially, "Being faithful and honest, is the master key." And then,
LOVE COMPLICATIONS. Honey chile!!! Remember, there's always light at
the end of the tunnel because the light shines from within you guiding your way!

Where are you writing us from? What's your take on the Poets Niche? Have
you received any positive comments from our members? Looking forward to
reading more of your poems, and glad that we have provided you a home to
showcase your poems.

always
moni

/~~~~~~\

Date: Monday, September 7, 1998
To: moni
From: ROSEFORMS
Subject: Website

Dear Moni:

I found out about your website after a friend of mine emailed me Walt's Friday
inspirations. I emailed Walt, telling him how much I liked his inspirational
message, and he sent me a link to the website. And as they say, "The rest is
history".

I think the Poets Niche is wonderful, and I am glad to be a part of it. I hope that
all of you will keep up the good work. I have enjoyed showcasing my work, and
I have REALLY enjoyed the works of the other poets.

Walt's "inspirations," have really helped me through some rough times lately.

Keep on with the keeping on,
Rose

49

```
/~~~~~~~~~~~~~~~~~~~~~~~~~~~~~~~~~~~~~~~~~~~~~~~~~~~~~~~~~~~~~~~~\
```
Date:	Monday, September 7, 1998
To:	Flite
From:	moni
Subject:	W E L C O M E

Dear Flite:

I have received all of your submissions, and I'm floored by the beauty and wisdom your poems evoke. If I had to pick a favorite one, however, IT WON'T BE LONG, seems to touch me more profoundly. BUT, then there's IT ONLY TAKES ONE SIP, which you should consider submitting to MADD (Mothers Against Drunk Drivers).

moni


```
/~~~~~~~~~~~~~~~~~~~~~~~~~~~~~~~~~~~~~~~~~~~~~~~~~~~~~~~~~~~~~~~~\
```
Date:	Tuesday, September 8, 1998
To:	moni
From:	Chris Hare
Subject:	Just who is Valentino

Hi Moni:

I'm writing you from Virginia. I got the name Valentino from some of my female co-workers when I was in the Marines. They joked that my eyelashes were unusually long for a man and that I used mascara to keep them that way. No, I don't use it, but I do brush them to keep them out of my eyes.

I am glad you liked my poem "The Lonely Diva". I got the inspiration from a documentary about young girls who have run away and ended up becoming prostitutes. Some of the mental blocks they have to use to get through the day or night. So far I have received favorable reviews and open arms into the Poets Niche. I just started reading some of the poems and they are pretty good! I am going to send my comments to some of the authors.

Most of my poems are from my own personal experiences and painful realizations. Poetry became an outlet for me. I guess you could say I go from one extreme to the next. From psychological to erotic, and all in between. Nothing disgusting, just thought provoking.

I think the Poets Niche is a great place, and I am glad that I found it. I ran across it while searching for information on various poetry contests. I had one of my poems published in their anthology. I will send it to you later if you would like to read it.

Thanks for your comments and allowing me to showcase my work.

Valentino

/~~~~~~\

Date:	Tuesday, September 8, 1998
To:	moni
From:	FLITE
Subject:	W E L C O M E

Thank you so much for your encouraging remarks. Your support really means a lot. May the peace and love of Jesus be with you,

FLITE

/~~~~~~\

Date:	Wednesday, September 9, 1998
To:	POETS NICHE
From:	MONI
Subject:	PADMORE

Two weeks ago Padmore received his MASTERS in African American Literature. And the BEST PART is he completed what is usually a two year program in 9 MONTHS!!!! A party was hosted in his honor by the Ghanaian community.

*****WAY TO GO PADMORE******

Currently, Padmore is enrolled in the Ph.D. program in English at Ohio State University. Our prayers, support and love to one of our own, PADMORE, as he works toward obtaining his Ph.D.!!!

From a little birdie!
moni

/~~~~~~\

Date:	Thursday, September 10, 1998
To:	moni
From:	Angela
Subject:	W E L C O M E

Hello Moni:

Sorry it took me so long to respond. Things have been pretty hectic around here.

Well, I bring you greetings from the windy city, Chicago. I heard about the website from my son's godfather, Shawn Goins. I found so many wonderful things there. I was like a kid in a candy store. I love the Poets Niche! I've been writing poetry since I was 13 years old. I shared my poems with friends in school, and with my family. I write poetry based on my own life experiences, and things that I observe. I enjoy writing, and sometimes I feel I express myself better on paper than I do verbally. I have my BA in English.

I've met some very interesting people from the Poets Niche, and I'm glad that I joined. I've met friends from all over and started communicating via email and sometimes by phone. I really appreciated the feedback I received regarding my poem, "Love Complications". I think that everyone could tell that it was an autobiography. The men from the Niche were especially supportive. The statement you made about the light shining within me guiding the way is similar to a statement I always use: "I have a light within me that no one can take away. It's my heart. If my light goes out, my heart will stop beating; and I'm not dead yet, so let me keep on shining!" Thanks for taking the time to read my poetry, and to personally welcome me. I look forward to hearing more from everyone, and sharing more.

Angela

```
/~~~~~~~~~~~~~~~~~~~~~~~~~~~~~~~~~~~~~~~~~~~~~~~~~~~~~~~~~~~~\
```

Date: Friday, September 11, 1998
To: moni
From: Katherine Smith
Subject: New member

Hi Moni!

I was referred by Chief Makanga for the shares*[*see editor's note below]*, and
when I e-mailed Walt for his Friday Inspirations. Because I write poetry, I
decided to join the Poets Niche.

I am a freelance writer in the Dallas, Texas and I have written three books. My
books are on Poetry, Humor and Self-Help. I have been published in "The
Morning Calm" - Korean Air's inflight magazine. I also write for The Black
Economic Times in Dallas, Texas.

I operate a company in which I write marketing materials for companies, and I
also have an "On-Line Business Resource Center" @ www.minorityres.org.

I am impressed with the site and I am glad to be a part of what you are doing.

Thanks

Katherine

**So much is happening! As a way to boost traffic to the site, I've set up a
"free share giveaway" that's attracting hundreds of people each day. At the
same time, friendships are developing among the members of the Poets Niche and
there seems to be a growing sentiment among us all that we'd like to meet each
other face toface.*
    *Another active member of our group, Pam Barnes sparked an idea for us
to arrange a gathering so we could do just that!*

```
/~~~~~~~~~~~~~~~~~~~~~~~~~~~~~~~~~~~~~~~~~~~~~~~~~~~~~~~~~~~~~~\
```

Date: Monday, September 14, 1998
To: Pamela Barnes
From: moni
Subject: OFFLINE PARTY

Hoping all is well with you. And, thanks for sending LeNora our way.

Regarding your suggestion for an OFFLINE PARTY, Pam you must've been
reading my mind (at least the part that's working). Walt and I discussed this very
thing several weeks ago -- a conference/meeting or as you put it, OFFLINE
PARTY of the Poets Niche.

As far as a location, time and place, here my suggestions:

1) Next summer in New Orleans around the same time as the Essence Festival
(July 2-5). This can either be planned before, during or just right after the
Essence Festival. It will allow our members to join in on the festivities that
Essence has to offer, see the sites in New Orleans, then meet and greet with the
Niche members.

2) Martha's Vineyard - Never been there but would love to go. Reservations at
some of the best bed-and-breakfast inns, and beautiful weather. I don't know
what they have going on in the months of July thru August, but you can check
with the Chamber of Commerce or Black Tourist Group for information. Again,
we can combine our conference with an event there and give our members a
double dose for their money.

3) Atlanta/Savannah, Georgia - My son lived there for 4 years and I thought the
City was lovely. A friend of mine is a writer/poet, lives in Savannah. He
manages a bookstore, and familiar with all the literary groups in the area. We
have a few members who live in Atlanta, who already belong to local poetry
groups and could be very helpful. Several years ago, I planned my Family
Reunion in Atlanta and had a blast!!

4) And last but not least, your neck of the woods, Dallas, Texas. My sister lived
in Dallas and Ft. Worth for years. And, since you are more familiar with the
pulse of the city, you can combine our conference with any upcoming events in
Dallas. Kinda like two for the price of one.

Since we have members from all over the country, selecting a location should be
a breeze. Finally, wherever it is decided we should host our first OFFLINE

PARTY, we should use this as an opportunity to market and sell the Poets Niche first anthology, COME INTO OUR WHIRL.

Pam, I'm glad you are enjoying connecting with our, as you put it, creative, unique, uplifting . . . God-Sent, members. Little did we know, even though we hoped, the Poets Niche would be so popular.

If you have a moment, please feel free to call me so we can discuss all of the above, or even better, just talk.

Until then,

from your extended family member/baby sister (HA).
moni

/~~~~~~\

Date: Tuesday, September 15, 1998
To: Katherine
From: moni
Subject: Your poem

Katherine:

I'll post your website on the Bulletin Board tomorrow.

Honey, chile, COLORED is the bomb!!! I especially love this:

> I am yellow
and pink
Flushed of my natural color
As a result of disease
In the minds of the greedy
and the hateful.

I THINK YOU ARE JUST TOO BADDD!!! I'd love to know what was going on in your head/life when you wrote this one.

As far as typos, gurl my life is just one big white-out after another. For example, I notified the members about Poems of the Week 6 being posted and said: DRUM ROLL PLEASE and TWO THUMPS UP FOR ..... "thumbbbbbbss" not "thumps" I said, AFTER I hit the send button to everyone. Well, that's just one more mistake to add to the list of many that God will erase when I cross those pearly gates.

You say you are shopping for a publisher. You may have found your "NICHE"!
Perhaps we can help you make your dreams come true. I'll have Walt contact/e-mail you about this.

Thanks for sending me COLORED, and please submit it to the group so everyone else can enjoy your poem too!!

Wishing you a lifetime of happiness,
moni

/~~~~~~\

Date:	Wednesday, September 16, 1998
To:	Katherine
From:	moni
Subject:	Plug away!

Moni:

Thank you, thank you, thank you!!! I really appreciate your support and encouragement. It takes a lot to finally step out on what you love to do and hope and pray that you can "reach" someone with the passion you possess. Thank you. I can't say it enough. I took your advice and shared my poems with the group.

Kat

/~~~~~~\

Date:	Wednesday, October 14, 1998
To:	moni
From:	Suli
Subject:	Re: Hello!!!!

Thanks for your note of greeting! I learned about The Poets Niche through John Riddick, who published a piece of my work. I have truly enjoyed the wonderful thoughts shared by the wonderful minds involved in this endeavor.

I write to you from Rockland, NY. I have received many kind thoughts from fellow 'niche-rs', and I am pleased to see their feelings and thoughts unfold before me on the screen. I had recently done some very erotic work as well as some romantic poems, which makes up the bulk of my time. I am interested in showing them to seasoned writers and getting feedback. (Which is why I like the Niche!)

My next personal step is to revamp my webpage, redo pics and the backgrounds. I'd like to see my work bound beautifully in a vanity printing in its entirety, and some more poems published of course!!)

Thanks again for your interest and your warm welcome into The Poets Niche Family!

Suli

As a mentor of mine is known to say: "It gets gooderer and gooderer!"

/~~~~~~\

Date: Wednesday, October 14, 1998
To: Poets Niche 1; Poets Niche 2; Poets Niche 3
From: moni
Subject: A MESSAGE FROM MONI

Dear Poets Niche Members:

There are very few people who affect my life so profoundly! Walt, is such a person. Walt's journal entry and Friday Inspiration No. 59, "Just Because I Am," was more than an inspiration for me -- it was a BLUEPRINT in believing in your own self-worth. The moment we are conceived, then born, we immediately inherit worthiness and everything that goes with it -- from the beginning until forever.

With the recent release of Walt's book "The Silent Performer," I now know why our paths crossed. He dried the tears he never knew I wept, and filled a void he never knew was empty.

With that in mind, I was compelled to write a little something about my friend. I hope he won't be too embarrassed.

always
moni

WHO IS WALT AND WHY?

Who Is Walt and Why?
First, I thought he was a spy, but
I quickly learned that Walt didn't lie.

Our initial contact may have been electronic,
but our meeting wasn't ironic.

I soon discovered that Walt is a lover.
A lover of mankind.
A lover of truth.
A lover of possibilities.
A lover of life's simple pleasures.

Who Is Walt and Why?
A man with a philosophy of "Do it
NOW because the FUTURE is HERE."
A man who THINKS IT, BELIEVES IT,
therefore, IT IS.

Who Is Walt and Why?
Walt's only desire is to see others inspired.
I'll just end this and say, Walt is my friend,
who gave ME the confidence to use my
wings to

F L Y

Monica D. Blache (c) 1998

/~~~~~~\

Date: Thursday, October 15, 1998
To: moni
From: Shenita
Subject: A MESSAGE FROM MONI

This is absolutely beautiful. Walt has made a positive impact in my life as well.
I am starting my own business as a Development Consultant (fund-raiser) and a
Special Events Coordinator -- which is my true passion. My days of thinking
that I must only do one thing are now over. Walt is truly a wonderful inspiration.
Thanks for your words... you have captured my feelings.

You are truly beautiful. Continue to fly... my sister. The world is ours!

Shenita a/k/a Queen

/~~~~~~\

Date: Thursday, October 15, 1998
To: moni
From: Ancient Tradition
Subject: A MESSAGE FROM MONI

A very honorable tribute Moni, it touched My heart...

Keep flying!

David

/~~~~~~\

Date: Thursday, October 15, 1998
To: moni
From: ROSEFORMS
Subject: A MESSAGE FROM MONI

You know it GURL!!!!! Until now, I thought I was Walt's biggest fan on the
'Niche'. Well, I see he has many. I love the piece. Keep up the good work!

Rose

```
/~~~~~~~~~~~~~~~~~~~~~~~~~~~~~~~~~~~~~~~~~~~~~~~~~~~~~~~~~~~~~~~\
```

Date: Wednesday, October 21, 1998
To: Poets Niche 1; Poets Niche 2; Poets Niche 3
From: moni
Subject: MONI'S HAVING TOO MUCH FUN!!!!!

DEAR FRIENDS!!!!

NO ONE TOLD ME IT WOULD BE THIS MUCH FUN!!!!!

Since our humble beginnings of the Poets Niche in late June, 1998, we have
received 250+ poems. What's even more incredible is that I get to read inspiring
and thought provoking poetry written by extremely gifted poets, over and over
again!!! (for the Poets Niche current anthology, COME INTO OUR WHIRL, and
future anthologies). I have learned so much from each and everyone of you. I
have also had the pleasure of meeting some interesting people, making new
friends, and even lucky enough to talk with many of you.

That being said, I started noticing at the end of some of my sister-friend, Rose
Ford's submissions, a saying "life ain't nothing but a series of words". Not only
did this strike me as a wonderful saying, but it perfectly described my life. I
emailed Rose to find out what "life ain't nothing but a series of words," meant, or
if it was a book (her book).

A couple of weeks ago, Rose was kind enough to send me two of her books, "life
ain't nothing but a series of words," and "Just when you thought it was safe, To
start reading poem books again". If you really want to know L. K. "Rose" Ford,
just read her books. I especially enjoyed, Pledging My Love; Did you See Me;
Halftime; and Wings (Part II). I know Rose wrote these books as a labor of love,
first for herself (the girl is always writing something), and then for others to
enjoy.

In a couple of weeks, I will post information on the Poets Niche Bulletin Board
on how you can order Rose's books online.

I'm having the best time of my life, and it's because of ALL OF YOU. Thanks
for making what I do for you so much FUN!!!

always
moni

Date: Monday, November 9, 1998 7:58
To: Poets Niche 1; Poets Niche 2; Poets Niche 3
From: moni
Subject: TEAMWORK = POEMS OF THE WEEK 11

Happy Monday All:

What Poets Niche member has collaborated with two other members of the Poets Niche and created a unique style of their own?

Clues: 1) The King _____ version of the Bible; and
        2) _____, England.

And, his collaborators both have the letter "T" as the first initial in their first name.

Check out POEMS OF THE WEEK 11 and find out who they are!!

If there is another member in the Poets Niche that you've been dying to "collaborate" with because of similar writing styles, or just for the fun of it, (like Rose Ford and David Weeks have done with "You Are My Lullaby"), team up and let us read your poems!!

always
moni

Date: Monday, November 16, 1998
To: moni
From: Pamela Barnes
Subject: MONI'S TOP 10

I like this moni -- You Go Girlllllllllllllllllllll!!!!!! (smile). I will have some information to send out to you about the upcoming Poets Niche First Annual Offline PARTY, "Come Into My Whirl," Summer '99 Party in HotLanta!! (A Party With A Purpose).

Pam

Date:	Monday, November 16, 1998
To:	moni
From:	Pamela Barnes
Subject:	MONI'S TOP 10

I have a feeling that you and I are going to be "tight" -- you are so much like me!! (that's scary).   I want to send out a survey to the Poet's Niche Family. I am so EXCITED!!!! We are going to have a blast!!! My boss is gone ALL WEEK...so you know what they say when the cat's away........

Pam

Date:	Thursday, November 19, 1998
To:	moni
From:	z_porterrc@XXX
Subject:	Hello from Robin

Moni:

I found out about the Poets Niche from my friend, James London. I told him I wanted to have a chance to read other poetry and perhaps submit mine. But now I've kinda gotten cold feet cause I don't like for people to use my unpublished pieces and claim them as their own. I'm working up to it. I hope to hear from you soon.

Robin

Date:	Monday, November 23, 1998
To:	moni; Poets Niche 1; Poets Niche 2; Poets Niche 3
From:	Pamela Barnes
Subject:	HotLanta Update

Hello everyone on this short week for most, if not all of us.....

Here's another brief survey:

1 - Although I had not asked yet, but many have already told me that the first

weekend in August would be excellent for the Offline Party. I checked with the Hyatt this morning and that weekend is open (so far). Thursday, August 5th arrival (by 6pm) and Sunday, August 8th departure. IF THIS IS AN OPEN WEEKEND FOR YOU....let me know ASAP!! (no later than 12/5/98)

2 - Discounts come in numbers, so advise me of HOW MANY WILL BE IN YOUR PARTY? This is for the hotel only, as I am letting everyone handle their own travel discounts. If quite a number of you are coming from a selected city on a selected day, check with the airline/travel agency for discounts. It never hurts to ask, and ask again, BOTH the airline and the travel agency!! Try to utilize a black travel agency, as we tend to try to look out for each other.

3 - Speaking of looking out for each other....I already got a "hook-up" (yall know we love hook-ups) via the Atlanta Black Heritage Bus Tour. I told her about US and she stated that she would give us the "Family Reunion discount" on the tickets.....regularly priced at $30, now $20. I'm using that same terminology "family reunion" for the hotels as well. I'm sure some of us look alike, at least that's what they say. (laugh) As far as I am concerned, all black people are related!!

4 - All in favor of T-Shirts and Caps, say "I". No need to send sizes....I'm making it simple "One Size Fits All". My brother and moni's son (two up-and-coming artists in New York) will be commissioned to design our shirts and caps for us. We're keeping it in the family!!

5 - I'm sure everyone will be taking pictures over the holidays....and with the idea of designing a souvenir/memory book from our adventures in HotLanta, I wanted to include everyone's picture with a bit of interesting data/facts about each of us to be a part of the book. I will need a good, clear headshot or full body shot (no nudies, please) to be sent to me eventually, so start striking some poses. I am also going to request the Mayor of HotLanta to send us a letter of proclamation declaring that weekend "Poets Niche Weekend", to be a part of the book, too. This information (picture and data) will be requested from you at a later date. I'll send you your data sheet after Thanksgiving to be completed and returned to me via snail mail.

Make sure you keep up with all of your e:mails regarding the Offline Party! One change has been made....the Soul Food Farewell Brunch. I overlooked the fact that many will be leaving on Sunday and the brunch will conflict with the hotel's check-out time, so the "soul food" will take place Saturday, instead of Sunday. Start saving, dieting, energizing NOW for in just a few months, we'll be painting the town red in HotLanta!!

More to Come!!! Happy Thanksgiving; and for those traveling, I am praying for your traveling grace.

Lagniappe (A Louisiana term meaning "extra")

In this season of giving.....

Too Blessed to be Stressed

Pam

/~~~~~~\

Date:	Wednesday, December 9, 1998
To:	Poets Niche 1; Poets Niche 2; Poets Niche 3
From:	moni
Subject:	MIDDLE OF THE WEEK RELIEF from moni

* HAPPY WEDNESDAY *
(Thanks doc! I'll have another one of those shots around NOON)

Please don't tell Walt about this email, because he'll take away my (lucky you have computer privileges missy).

Walt and I struggled (more like battled) over the title of WHO THE HECTIC IS MONI? or WHO THE HECK IS MONI? Because I have a hectic schedule (at home eating brownies, watching the soaps, while getting a full body massage), Walt wanted to go with WHO THE HECTIC IS MONI? I, on the other hand, said because everyone's been trying to figure out who I am (A SAINT, of course) let's go with WHO THE HECK IS MONI? Therefore, we compromised (really Walt won because he's the technical brains, and I'm using my last marble for this email).

Here's where you guys come in. Please tell us which title you prefer:

MONI'S - WHO THE HECK IS MONI? (vote for me and I promise
NO MORE TAXES until I have to break my promise)
or
Walt's - WHO THE HECTIC IS MONI? (let him make his own deals)

In the meantime, and as promised in moni's top 10, checkout the Poets Niche website and find out WHO THE HECTIC IS MONI? or WHO THE HECK IS MONI?

always working hard to make this a safe place for poets to write (my campaign platform)! --moni

Date: Wednesday, December 9, 1998
To: moni
From: Pamela Barnes
Subject: MIDDLE OF THE WEEK RELIEF

Campaign Promises? Moni, I guess the next thing you'll want is an intern in a blue suit!! Vote for Moni!!

Pam

~~~~~~

Date: Wednesday, December 9, 1998
To: moni
From: Shenita
Subject: MIDDLE OF THE WEEK RELIEF

My vote is "WHO THE HECK IS MONI". Ok? I said it, it should be a done deal now!

Peace

Queen

~~~~~~

Date: Wednesday, December 9, 1998
To: moni, Poets Niche
From: Chris Hare
Subject: Missing in action

Hello fellow poets, if I can still be a member of the family. I know I have been absent from contributing to the flow of brilliance being expressed in the form of poetic thought. But, I have had my hands full with work and my mind has not been in the writing mode for a while. Although I did manage to take advantage of an opening in this mental block I have been experiencing to write this bit of life's reality.

Dear sweet sister moni, please accept my apology for leaving you and the rest of the family in the dark as to my well being. The time that has passed has given me something to think about. That is where this piece of literature evolved from. I hope all enjoys. As always comments are welcomed.

```
/~~~~~~~~~~~~~~~~~~~~~~~~~~~~~~~~~~~~~~~~~~~~~~~~~~~~~~~~~~~\
```

Date: Wednesday, December 9, 1998
To: Rose and bams
From: moni
Subject: TWO ROSES

Rose and bams!!

How could I be sooooo lucky to know 2, count them, 2 -- wonderful poets named
ROSE!!! Big Rose, I love your tribute to lil rose!! This is a prime example of
what the Poets Niche is all about - love and support of fellow members.

mad love for u both!

moni


```
/~~~~~~~~~~~~~~~~~~~~~~~~~~~~~~~~~~~~~~~~~~~~~~~~~~~~~~~~~~~\
```

Date: Wednesday, December 9, 1998
To: moni; ROSEFORMS
From: MsBam
Subject: Wow!!

/bams--for once, speechless


```
/~~~~~~~~~~~~~~~~~~~~~~~~~~~~~~~~~~~~~~~~~~~~~~~~~~~~~~~~~~~\
```

Date: Tuesday, January 5, 1999
To: moni
From: love eternal
Subject: More info please.....

Moni:

The Offline party sounds great!!!! You know I'll be there!!! If there is anything
you guys want me to do let me know I'm available Monday, Wednesday &
Friday after 1:00pm and all day Tuesday, Thursday, Saturday & Sunday (all other
times I'm in school). It's gonna be off da hook!!!!

Peace
Tasha

Date: Tuesday, January 12, 1999
To: Poets3@nichemarket.com
From: Rodney Coates
Subject: Deep Within My Nothingness

My brothers and sisters, welcome to the new year. I have spent the first of this New Year being refreshed in Ghana. While there I was inspired to write several poems, so please enjoy...this one...new for 99.
rodneyc.

Date: Tuesday, January 12, 1999
To: Poets Niche 1; Poets Niche 2; Poets Niche 3
From: moni
Subject: birthday wishes from moni

JUST SO YOU KNOW!
I've been brought up on charges by the BIRTHDAY PATROL PAROLE BOARD (try saying that three times), because of my investigative skills (more like back alley antics). And even though I used my OWN lunch money (money laundering scheme) to get this information, I must admit (or take the Fifth) it was worth it. HERE'S WHY!

WORD ON THE STREET is SUSAN HARRIGAN is celebrating a BIRTHDAY TODAY!! She is not BLU nor does she have MIXED EMOTIONS (Poems of the Week(s) 9 & 17) about turning ANOTHER YEAR OLDER!! She's just grateful my paid informant didn't tell me her AGE! YOU GOOOOO GURL, AND PARTY LIKE IT'S NINETEEN NINETY NINE (her real age).

Also turning another CHAPTER in his LIFE is not just another REVELATION for PADMORE AGBEMABIESE. But his FEELINGS ON AN AUTUMN NIGHT (Poems of the Week(s) 6, 13 & 18) is reason enough to pray to the God of Sun to melt away all the snow in Ohio. PADMORE, if you are looking for your birthday cake, the librarian said it's in the reference section under HAPPY BIRTHDAY!! (Padmore is always in the library studying because he is a Ph.D. candidate at Ohio State).

Wishing our sister, SUSAN HARRIGAN, and our brother, PADMORE AGBEMABIESE * HAPPY BIRTHDAY *
from your family at the POETS NICHE!!

much love moni

```
/~~~~~~~~~~~~~~~~~~~~~~~~~~~~~~~~~~~~~~~~~~~~~~~~~~~~~~~~~~~~~~\
```
Date: Thursday, January 14, 1999
To: moni
From: Mocha
Subject: The Poets Niche Website is tight!!

Moni:
I'm so proud of you. The Poets Niche website is EXCELLENT! I can't believe
all the things that have been added. As Brandy would say, we are truly "sitting
on top of the world".
Peace, Mocha

```
/~~~~~~~~~~~~~~~~~~~~~~~~~~~~~~~~~~~~~~~~~~~~~~~~~~~~~~~~~~~~~~\
```
Date: Thursday, January 14, 1999
To: Poets Niche 1; Poets Niche 2; Poets Niche 3
From: Pamela Barnes
Subject: OFFLINE PARTY PRESS RELEASE

FROM THE HEAD OFFICE!!

First Mike, now ME!! My fellow sistahs and brothas "COME INTO MY
WHIRL" tomorrow, as I make a major announcement. No, I can't be like Mike
and retire just yet.....but the long awaited information on the forthcoming Poets
Niche Offline Party in Hotlanta, Georgia, August 5th-8th will be released tomor-
row. Details from my press conference will be viewed via your EMAIL tomor-
row evening. Between all of the microphones and the cameras flashing tomor-
row, I'll give you all the information you have been awaiting.

The only thing I ask is that once this information is received, start acting on it
IMMEDIATELY!! You will receive a lot of information with DEADLINE
DATES. Please adhere to these dates!! Let's make this a stress-free event,
before, during, and after, okay?

As of today you now have 6-1/2 months to get those thighs firm and those
tummies tucked to show-off those 6-packs this summer. Get in the living room
this weekend and start learning and practicing the latest dance steps, however if
you feel like packing some of those old skool moves to bring with you, we won't
be mad at ya! Start searching catalogs and magazines for the latest in swimming
attire, the latest in hairstyles, etc.....this event comes with a "get your groove
back" guarantee. No money is going to have to be refunded -- I'm making sure of
that by planning every detail as carefully as possible!!

Until tomorrow......... PAMELA BARNES

Chapter Four

POETRY BY

POETS NICHE MEMBERS

==
Padmore Enyonam Agbemabiese
==

PADMORE ENYONAM AGBEMABIESE -
Padmore was born in Ghana. He is a poet, playwright, scholar and a renowned journalist. His poems confront readers with the rhythmic intensity of traditional imageries that call on the reader to undertake an introspective examination of the self and the world he or she inhabits. His poems also deal with issues of race, gender cum the economic and political throes that entangle not only Africa but the sons and daughters of Africa, at large.

AFRICA

Dear Mother,
this story is a song sang
into minds....our minds, your
mind, her mind, his mind....it
speaks of nothing new; it is old, but it is new.

This letter, it speaks of tears
of mothers crying
for their sons falling
by the wretched sea; it speaks of scars
carried long,
long on the heart, on the mind.

And everywhere I go I
stumble on these scars. It is
on the breast of the ocean, on the streets
of the sky, under the armpit of the
wind. It is on the face of our smiles.

It confronts me, you, he, she,
night and day, moon and shine,
dripping blood in every space.

They stand in the shadow of the
rivers, stroll on roads to the golf course.

They shoot pathetic death
into loins, firing musketry
into minefields.

We dress them for
the table, for postmortem,
and we weep floods
for flames sparked in
Mississippi, Oklahoma,
Alabama, Soweto, Burundi, Rwanda.

They shred our dreams to dirges
our festival to nightmares, dine flames
into our eyes...our minds....our arms....

You need not come
with me down this road to hear

we die.........hungry free men

homeless sons of Malcolm X,
King Jr., Marcus Garvey, Lumumba,
Kwame Nkrumah, and I remember
the kingdom without your children.

And we fade, we fade,
fade into arms of Guns and
Roses...gunsgunsgunsgunsguns
and we fade.

Have we not
lost Toussaint, Macandal,
Lumumba to the savage
haste of gnomic gods? What
about the profiteering
angels?

Did you hear the
wife of the Circus Manager, Rome
rode the mule to the market?
We bought the viruses in
the restaurants, in the grocery
shops, and at school
we read our names
from the bottom to the top of the page.

There were men without
names, even, in the telephone directory.

Who remembers then wives
bereft of husbands, women weeping,
mothers wailing for sons falling
to the hangman, daughters
lost to a wretched Sea that washed
shores long, long ago? It is a story not
told in history, nor read in books,

nor remembered in memories.
And this story speaks of time
not named; nor quoted by lips
to you, me, he, she, and we.

And these eyes get widened
to dress another skin.
Tell them from me
"We all are children of AFRICA".

==================================
Padmore Enyonam Agbemabiese
==================================

OUR PRAYERS

I dreamt again last night
one of those magic dreams
of childhood; amicable dreams
tall enough to make you laugh
It began like you always spoke
of our destinies always close

each day each minute
you compose private songs
of a small romance
in unclassifiable flowers
your lips to mine in faster dance
hemmed a world two lovers shared

I remember the dream again tonight
where I, was a boy climbing hills running
to incite timelessness in longings
there were mornings of promises
silver moons in broad daylight
close to a world of no droughts

Then the dream changed
like owls calling, haunting treetops
like cold rains wounding the green grass
I could not speak your language
your songs could not stay to be a witness
mine was a cautioning voice

I saw the world shared by two lovers
inhabited by a stormy weather
it was without a rainbow
I saw a dream out there
it did not have your face in it
your name isn't the name anymore

I had a wish written on my heart
it was not waiting for you
I saw a star so bright in the night
it couldn't be bright for your sight
there were songs everywhere
but they were not for your lips

there was strength enough
to wheel on
it was not enough for you
to depend on
it was like Romans invaded the peninsula
we were buried in separate continents

I remember the dream again this morning
one of those magic dreams
of childhood; amicable dreams
tall enough to make you laugh
It ended like you always spoke
when I go finding some new play

======================================
Padmore Enyonam Agbemabiese
======================================

PROPHECY

One day some day
I will claim my wings
I will seize the skies
I will take the land.

One day some day
I will return your heart home
to marry your soul to the land
the land of your father's birth
you will return to the land
where poems of love grow
from ribbons of human touch and there
you'll drink from pools of human laughter
and gather dreams of amazing grace.

One day some day I will return
loaded with hopes for dreams
return with the fiery of Sakpana
spit into the seasons of the Cobra

I'll step on mounds of burning chaos
pick maggots hanging on mouths
crush the lies in living museums
and the fury of Shango won't die

till the long tales of memory take pride
till them that weep gather smiles
till them that mourn sing new songs
in the land of their father's birth.

....Padmore is currently a Ph.D. English candidate at Ohio State University. He has published two volumes of Ewe poetry together with academic essays, and articles in international magazines. He has to his credit four unpublished plays, famous among them is DZAKPATA, which runs yearly in the University of Ghana, Legon Staff and Students Production at the School of Performance Theater. He has won a number of awards for his creative works including the GWEN KAGEY AWARD, 1998, FOR HIGH ACADEMIC ACHIEVEMENT at Ohio State University.

```
===================================
'bams
===================================
```

in tender days
{"dear mama"}

her gait no longer has
the power of twenty
providing fuel to it
her house, no longer
ruled by iron fist
the laughter of children
peals only temporarily
from grown-old walls

{i tell you now}

where there were once nine
there are now none
none but her
still she says
she's not lonely
though alone

{i say to you}

the silver strands
she wished for/she earned
streak naturally through
her natural hair
(and i am quite sure that
i put a few strands there)

{and yet}

and yet, when--
God in her--
she does the happy dance,
i am pleased to report
she has not missed a beat

ROSE /bams COOPER

*WifeMotherDaughterLover
StorytellerAdventurerBikerSeeker.*

*That, and more; Rose /
bams Cooper is a work-
in-progress. More a
storyteller than a writer,
her poems and prose tell
the story of an ordinary
woman living an
extraordinary life. Hailing
from Detroit, Michigan,
she now lives in Lansing
Fun City, USA with her
husband Michael Bear
Cooper and their two
boys; check us out at
http://manetheren.cl.msu.edu/
~bambam/*

```
=====================================
/bams
=====================================
```

the all-purpose poem, generic aisle no.1
  (dedicated to my fellow niche-ers)

"ACCESSIBLE! ACCESSIBLE!",
the agent said to me;
"Make your poems ACCESSIBLE!
to those who cannot read!"

  to those who cannot read? i asked,
   my eyes and mind agape;
"ACCESSIBILITY! is all!"
he mimicked, like an ape.

"Trust me, dear child," he said to me,
"Trust me, because, you see,
your writing is too damned complex--
it requires folks to read."

  at this, i looked at him as if
  he had just pulled himself up outta the spin cycle.

  he continued on:

"And if you make them read," he said
"It might drive them to drink.
For reading poetry's a pain--
it requires folks to think."

  uh, no sh-t, sherlock. but, being polite,
  i kept my True Feelings to myself
  for the time being. hell, he's Literate.
  he knows of whence he speaks. right? hmmm.

  so, what do you suggest? i asked,
   (though I didn't wanna know);
"ACCESSIBILITY!, the key,
I'll tell you what should go."

"The first to go should be the way
you space and type your words;
those little letters are too small,
your spacing's for the birds!"

"And while you're at it," he did say,
"why don't you make it rhyme?
I learned in grade school that is how
poetry's done most the time!"

   by this point, i'm wondering to myself
   whether or not he got his Literary Agent Badge
   from a box of crackerjacks. but hell, he's on a roll,
   let him finish. maybe i'll Learn Something.

"I've got another good suggestion!"
he went on to voice;
"I'd give up being Deep, my dear;
but, really, it's your choice."

"All-in-all, I would remove
the differences you scribe;
ACCESSIBILITY!--utmost--
means setting them aside."

   y b nermal? i asked him.
He answered with a "tut!
An abeynermal attitude
will land you on your butt!"

"You said you want to get paid, yeah?"
he teased, knowing my plight;
"Well, if you do, the only way
is writing Poetry-Lite."

   of course, i vamoosed. so who needs money, anyway?

```
========================================
```
/bams
```
========================================
```

ghetto pets

hey, ma!
    pookie on tha corner
    came to baaro some sugar
t'day

but, ma--
    pookie on tha corner
    said he aint gon come back
this way

cuz, ma,
    pookie on tha corner
    screamt at all our roaches
and rats

and ma,
    pookie on tha corner
    said that NORMAL peeples
keep cats!

hmmm...ma?
    pookie on tha corner's
    house is just like ours is,
right?

and, ma,
    pookie on tha corner's
    house seems REAL allergic
to light...

mmmm...ma?
    pookie on tha corner's
    clothing always seems like
it crawls

plus, ma,
    pookie on tha corner's

house got hoofprints all up
tha walls

when, ma,
    pookie on tha corner's
    mama tried to send him
to camp

then, ma,
    pookie on tha corner's
    mama paid for it
wif stamps!

so, ma?
    pookie on tha corner
    got no room dog US out,
eh?

so, ma,
    pookie on tha corner
    kin kiss US black ass
ok?

        ow, ma, why you do dat?

"My creative
energies as of late are
focused toward
publishing two books of
poetry, titled BAMMER'S
GROOVE: Petals And
Thorns, and Many
Voices. I'm also working
on three anthologies of
(true) short stories
simultaneously, simply
titled Love Stories,
Mother's Stories, and
Child's Stories. By the
way, my nickname
BamBam (/bams) isn't
from The Flintstones; I'm
a drummer, y'see..."

Dorothy Benner

==

Dorothy Benner

==

DOROTHY BENNER

Dori is a 43-year old single mom of three children and grand-mother of two. She is a full-time nurse in a nursing home and finds it to be both trying and rewarding. She began writing poetry in junior high school as a release for pent-up emotions, and has not stopped yet.

DON'T

We cling to each other,
Like logs after a shipwreck,
In a vast sea of despair,
So afraid of being alone,
Yet not really ready,
To trust ourselves wholly,
One to the other.
Love is a word,
That comes too easy to our lips,
Yet the meaning is empty.
Don't hold me so tight.....
But, please don't let me go.

==

Dorothy Benner

==

LOSS OF INNOCENCE

We were children,
Patriotic, brave children,
Innocent of Horror.
All too soon,
We were forced to grow up,
To face danger and bloodshed..
Terrors real and imagined,
Waited there in the dark.
But grimly determined,
We stood our ground,
Though the reason got lost,

In the fight.
And we were Proud!
Then we came home...
Some of us whole and some of us not,
And no one cared.
All these years, we've stumbled along,

Bewildered and lost, remembering and lonely...
Scorned, ridiculed and ignored,
For something out of our control.

And now we're men,
Hardened and inside ourselves,
But it's not too late,
Won't you try to understand?
We were just children.

Dori loves to learn new things, which explains her many hobbies — cross-stitching, plastic canvas, arts and crafts, reading, writing poetry and short stories.

She was recently engaged to a great guy, Mike. Her future plans include retirement (someday), planting a garden, getting published, and winning the Pulitzer.

===================================

Sandra Bushell

===================================

SANDRA BUSHELL

Sandi currently lives in the mountains of North Carolina with her two young children. When she was 12, she was encouraged by a teacher to continue writing poetry and stories after she won first place for her first prose piece. She has had different pieces published on the Web in sites such as: The CBStar Ezine, CrystalOasis Ezine, The Rose and Thorn Literary Ezine, and various webpages designed for poets. She has a degree in Nuclear Technology, and is a chat host for AOL dealing with metaphysical topics.

Wrinkles In Time

A glitch out in space
Causes time to erase
Courses that were so defined
A rogue wind so blows
And the direction it chose
Made a connection with no reason or rhyme

Their two paths separately
Maintained evenly
Paralleled the lives they have led
But for the wrinkle in time
Causing their roads to entwine
They have woven together instead

A millisecond of thought
Brought her what she sought
Through all the debris of her years
He looked in to find
That a wrinkle in time
Brought him past his mistrust and fears

They are still encased
in the past, words are chased
'Round about in the memories so scarred
Trust builds everyday
Mounting an offensive, so to say
That can heal the emotions so marred

Maybe a blink or a sneeze
Made the timeline appease
A cycle that was destined to connect
Their different lifetimes
With similar life crimes
Saw unknown hands that point and direct

A mist fogs the mind,
Does away with staid time,

Making a mockery of conventional clocks.
They notice the dates
Not believing that fate
Gave them each other in so short a block

It wonders her mind
That a wrinkle in time
Brought her this man that she loves to be near
She warms to his touch
And to his caring, so much
Her doubts are evaporated with her fear

He still has not defined
That little wrinkle in time
That cast him into her heart
But he nestles so close
And his heart has a hope
That no one can drive them apart

For now, you can see
That we, you and me
Have a gratitude to offer above
For that wrinkle in time
Gave to us, each other to find
And the beginnings of a new way to love

======================================
Sandra Bushell
======================================

Speak to Me

Speak to me of love, my poet
Let your rhyming words weave their spells
Cadence and timing beat within my breast
Lilting phrases soar with my thoughts of you
Emoting expressions, enigma wrapped,
telling what is deep in your heart

Sing to me of love, my poet
Let those words flow from the music of your soul
Your soft melody offered for my harmonies
Your quiet ways making me vibrate with the rhythms
Caressing my heart with your poignant notes

Whisper to me of love, my poet
Voice husky and deep, like our moments after lovemaking
Arm encircles me, I become an extension of you
Joined at the moment of mutual release,
Well timed murmurings met with the pregnant sighs

Touch me with love, my poet
Giving gently caring phrases that rivet my thoughts
My body a blank sheet to capture the treasured imagery
Penning every inch with your special perfection
Refining and defining every syllable, every pause

Write to me of love, my poet
Words filling the page unrestricted by a chained heart
Exposing a side rarely seen from behind the shield
An offering on a gold tray for untrained minds to ponder
The precious gems sparkling radiantly, illuminating minds

Think of me as love, my poet
A sweet rendering that gives you laughter and peace
Not empty as first believed, but nurtured, tended with grace
Built upon the tiny seeds of quest...watered with saline tears
growing mighty with your warmth, flowering under your touch

Listen to my love, my poet
Scales and bars are my forte, a melody sung for your pleasure
Music swells to a crescendo, voice singing clearly, serene
Fingers fretting, fluttering over the varied notes to accompany
Eyes dropped, emotionally rich expressions harbored in a song

Look closely at my love, my poet
Examine it under your exacting microscopic gaze
Find any fissures, any weakening in my wall of desires
Inspect the reasons, dissect the intricate workings of my heart
Remember how the feelings were built, and know the soundness

Fill your heart with my love, my poet
Steel-lined empty chambers hardened with pain
My furnace fired touch melting the scarred lining
Bringing a new warmth that drives away the cold
giving a piece of my own heart to repair ravages of time...

Read this verse of love, my poet
Written for you from one not as gifted
humbly offered to relate our pasts and futures
words scribed for you, first times becoming next times
Every time a mystery...overtime miraculous........

Because...of you...

Taheba Byrd
==

A New Look on Life

How do you know when it's real
Is it simply how you feel?
When do you say good-bye
When you tire of all the lies?
Do you run around with your emotions out of tac
Or do you stick to the rules/guidelines and facts?
Do you smile to a passer-by.
Or wait to see if someone else would say hi!
As you see as life grows more intense.
And you start to put up your defense.
The walls around you may be made of stone.
And your qualities and uniqueness go unshown.
How is it that you are free?
But you are hiding who you are and not letting me be me.
Well, break the shell and take down the invisible walls.
And learn and live and live and love
And let your personality grow strong.
As you know you have one life to live
But it depends on what you are willing to give.

TAHEBA BYRD

Taheba means "Sunshine". She has a 10-year old daughter, Brianna, who is also a poet! She started writing songs and short stories seventeen years ago. Then as her life turned into different chapters, poetry became her lifeline between reality and fantasy.

==
Taheba Byrd
==

This is the year

This is the place to turn a new leaf
Start a new race
1999 is finally here
Let down my worries and cast down all fears
This is my time to shine
Sound the alarms
For this year I have declared as mine
Watch me as I grow
For one thought one day that I wouldn't show
OR step up to the plate
See I already knew I had the key to the gate

I will release the wisdom that has built within
All my years of holding back
Now are gone
Now is the time for me to break the shell
Jump out of the norm
Move from where I dwell
Shout it out for now I am here
As all of my past life suddenly disappears
For now I am completely free
Why it took me to 1999 is totally beyond me!

"..... My poems are the windows to my world, and those who read them share pieces of my life. I give all my thanks for creativity to God, Jesus Christ!"

Angela Jones-Carr

Soul Searching

Life is playing games with my mind,
I can't seem to find my way.
I'm looking for something I can't seem to find,
I'm looking for a brighter day.

With each passing day, another dream drowns,
and I go on another whimsical journey.
My sun eclipses, and my smiles become frowns,
I start to dislike being me.

Life has me caught up in an unusual situation.
My life is so disturbed and complex.
It's filled with endless chaos and aggravation.
I don't know what's coming next.

My mind says stop though my body keeps going.
I'm getting tired of running this race.
The tension is rising, and confusion is growing.
I can't seem to find my place.

I fall to my knees and look to the skies,
"Lord anoint this lost child."
He embraces my soul, and wipes my eyes.
"My child, I was here all the while."

ANGELA JONES-CARR

Angela is a Chicago native where she is a telephone banker. She and husband Alonzo, have three children, Ticina, Alonzo Jr., and Jibri. Each one of them tells a story about her life.

"I owe my talent to God, from whom all of my blessings flow. I also love my parents for always being supportive and encouraging me to reach for the stars. I have also been blessed with a host of supportive and loving family members and friends...."

====================================
Angela Jones-Carr
====================================

Love Complications

> "Writing is my way of expressing my feelings, my fears, and my desires. "

As a child, it's a fairy tale;
As a teen, it's infatuation;
As a adult, it's one endless complication.

As a child I read about knights in shining armor,
I thought this would be the man I would marry.
As a teen, I thought I knew love,
but found infatuation quite scary.

Now I'm all grown up, not sure if I should believe.
Love is tearing me apart, and making me crazy.
It seems like all my bubbles have burst,
All of my sunshine is now hazy.

I've been lied to, beaten, and cheated on.
I've been talked about, used, and scorned.
I've been manipulated, and persuaded.
My heart is constantly torn.

They've tried stripping me of my self-esteem,
Tried to take away my pride.
They've tried to make me hang my head low,
feeling I should run and hide.

Is this all that love has to offer me?
Should I become as hard as stone?
Should I become the b--ch they're calling me,
or should I stay high upon my throne?

I have a baby girl that looks up to me,
I have to steer her right.
Do I tell her of love so fair,
or tell her of my plight?

As I dig down into my soul,
I find beauty no one can take away.

I find a woman fit for a king,
A strong, intelligent, black woman, to their dismay.

I am the creator's child,
He walks with me through the struggles of life.
Now, I no longer feel alone and confused,
He made me a wise mother, and loving wife.

....Angela began writing poems to recite at church at the age of 6. In high school she realized her true talent.

"I wrote lots of love poems at that time, and everyone wanted me to write a poem so that they could give them to their boyfriends."

She enjoyed writing so much that she majored in English at Loyola University in Chicago.

"I tend to write about things that are on my mind, things that have affected my life, or the lives of those around me. My poetry tells the story of my life. Writing is my way of expressing my feelings, my fears, and my desires. I also write short stories, and I hope to one day write a novel."

Rusty Knight

Helmet nothing but a Dent,
Torn, Ragged, Old Knight,
Spirit Worn, Hope Bent,
Not an inspiring sight.

Call me Rusty,
My Breastplate, dinged and split,
Campaigned, Dusty,
Chain mail, ragged and rent.

But what my eyes have seen
The battles borne, the body scarred.
And where I've been,
The rifts, rents I've fixed, darned.

Yes my eyes are hard
My lips thin
Laugh lines my countenance marred,
Yes, I've loved now and then.

My Sword nicked but straight,
The scabbard plain.
I've borne anger, and survived hate,
Tears shed, hidden in the rain.

I've walked and felt the cold,
Endured heat,
And, yes, I feel so damned old.
But my heart, still it beats.

A Rusty, Tired, Old Knight,
Campaigned and wise,
I am not a great grand sight.
But I've seen the sunrise.

SHAUN CECIL

Shaun was born in Texas, but currently lives in Oklahoma. His greatest accomplishment is being a father to Julian, Andrew and Rebecca. Shaun is a Paramedic/Fire Fighter and teacher who enjoys people......

Rusty, Tired, Rock Steady,
Here I stand,
Wait by me, for I am ready.
Here, take my hand.

Helmet nothing but a dent,
The Breastplate dinged and split.
But the Heart inside is not spent,
Beating loving, never ever quit.

======================================

Shaun Cecil

======================================

AGAIN

I could not fathom
Or really imagine,
That this would happen
Again.

I thought I had learned,
Since last I was spurned
And swore I'd never be burned
Again.

I read the right book,
Worked on my look,
But someway I got took
Again.

They say to never love
Is a sin against God above,
But is that reason enough to love
Again?

So I'll take my love to town,
And I will be bound,
If I ever see you around
Again!

".....I love Carl Sandburg, Elizabeth Barrett Browning and several others. I write poetry as a stress relief. My poetry has allowed me to meet some very special people involved with the Poets Niche (and they KNOW who they are)."

=====================================
TINA MARIE CLARK
=====================================

A BLACK MAN

He knows better times are coming
even if they're nowhere in sight
how can he win the battle? He needs
something in which to fight.

Let him enjoy his freedom, take away
those invisible chains, when will happiness
replace worry which invades his brain?
When he's mistreated he's asked to understand.

Well mountains aren't molehills, pleasure isn't
pain. He's truly a special person, I've witnessed
his traits, time and time again. Who you ask
 is this hero? He's A Black Man!

TINA MARIE CLARK

Tina Marie lives in New
Orleans, Louisiana, with
her husband of nineteen
years, Herbert, and two
sons, Prince and Joseph.
However, her nurturing
doesn't stop there
because she is also a
neighborhood mom.

Tina Marie is a poet and
songwriter. She has
written over 300 poems
and 200 plus songs.

TINA MARIE CLARK

LITTLE BLACK GIRL

This too is your world, you're more
precious than diamonds or pearls, so
wipe those eyes, don't you cry, everything's
gonna be just fine, remember you have a good
heart, you were born smart. You will win if you
believe in yourself. If you don't neither will
anyone else.

Hold back your tears find solutions instead, when
walking hold high your head, focus on achieving
don't be afraid, be proud of your color, which is
never second to any other!

For you are a supreme being, hold tight to your
dreams, if by this world you are never spoiled
you're already blessed to be A Little Black Girl!

===================================
Rodney Coates
===================================

Old School Love

Back in the day, when we were free,
waiting to walk you home....

So we walked, talked,
the road ahead just promises of things to come.
Fun, blue jeans, ice cream and you
. . . style, grace and flair were everything.

We lived, back then!
Breezy nights....
Soft caresses, silent moments and deep thoughts....
Hot kisses, cool talk ....

Telephone for you - it's that girl again!

....and much hope -- old school love.
Sitting on the couch,
hoping Mama doesn't see me kissing you.

Heavy breathing, tv rag,
fevered feelings, radio jams,
pointed debates about nothing/everything.......

Our future, the struggle, our past,
our today's great movie....

You kids all right in there?
It's awful quiet!

Sitting up straight.... the night; joy and pain;
hot buttered soul; popcorn and old school love.

RODNEY COATES

Rodneyc. is the pen name for Dr. Rodney D. Coates, who is the Director of Black World Studies and an Associate Professor of Sociology at Miami University Oxford, Ohio. He has been writing poetry for over 10 years, with his poetry being published in such publications as Obsidian, The Black Scholar, and many other literary magazines and newsletters.....

A walk around the hood,
arm-in-arm.......
riding our bikes when we could.

Continued.....
Listening, children played each other's heart;
thoughts, dreams, and schemes...

Shoulders, laughter, head held high;
Strutting our stuff, cool lives, warm hugs.

My Girl;
I got Sunshine;
Dream Lover....

Y'all be careful out there!

Staying out waaaay past midnight!
Tight pants; tough decisions; strong hands;
hope engaged in an old school love.

Deep river Johns, Mississippi dreams,
sidelong stares....kisses replacing life's cares.

Front yard love;
Back seat affairs;
hot steamy windows...
watching 3-D at the drive-in.

Filling spaces;
bumpy rides;
worn tires....
created under star-filled skies,
beckoning towards dawn.
Uplifting,
spiritual healing.......

Be back before midnight, you hear!

Life's troubled souls....
Souls music; enchanted dreams;
dayscapes and you
- my old school love....

Sunshine, brown eyes,
bountiful valleys of blue skies and
you.

Freely engaged,
raptured hearts uplifted into heaven's gaze.

Carefully placed,
timeless games and puberty's chains of despair.

With these hands.......

Does he have a job?

I'll cling to you, honor you!

Commitment, trust,
honestly engaged....that old school love!

Between the dreams, our plans pursued,
in the mix....

Captives of the moment....
Servants of love steeped in the pool of life.
Joy-filled, skylarks heralding the dawn.
Care abandoned....
Riding past our stop.
Righteous confessions.......
But, Mom we didn't do nothing!

Good-bye for now.......
Memories,
pleasant dreams of another day.
A clear sky and an old school love.

Deep-River love!
Higher than a Georgia-Pine love!
Honey-Dipped love!
Brick-House love!
Hearts Desire, Mind Boggling
Liberating love!

Stay this while....
Girl, why you wanna make me blue?

Dance with me!
With this life,
gone so soon....
I'll dedicate to you
- my old school love....

====================================

Rodney Coates

====================================

Road of No Return

Slow - beat the drums
from long ago and a
distant shore - lost in the
memory of misery.

Silent -flows the tears of
mothers, fathers,
sons, daughters - stolen
in the middle of their morning.

Dark - is the tunnel, down
that passage, through the
portal to this continuous night of despair.

Angry - shouts the walls
floors stained with blood dried
centuries ago by those whose
silent screams yet fills the void.

Thick - listen to the air crying out
their names, smell their souls
poured out into the mist as
a million souls blended with a million
dreams, blends with a million lost on
the road of no return.

> "My task: to bring sight to the blind, to heal wounds of affliction, and to set captives free. This is what I was called to do, and poetry is my vehicle. Thanks for allowing my words to find a place in your soul."
> --Rodney Coates
>
> A substantial collection of Rodney's work can be found at the following internet website (www.ulbobo.com/umoja/).

==
Mocha (B. Afena Cobham)
==

MOCHA
(B. AFENA COBHAM)

Mocha, the oldest of two children and the proud daughter of William and Louise Cobham, was born on Loring Air Force Base in Limestone, Maine and raised in East New York, Brooklyn. Her family relocated back to the south in the early 90's and currently resides in Atlanta, Georgia, which she too considers home base.....

Blank Pages: A Black Woman's Voice

A play on words is how I choose to fill the Blank Pages of life.
I write about my dreams, love and people who cause me strife.
The lines on this page are analogies to this complex world, in this
Pulitzer Prize kingdom; I'm the Queen blowing the literary minds
of every boy and girl.

The white paper serves as the canvas of my heart's spoken word.
For anyone else to be the author of my Blank Pages would truly
be absurd!

```
====================================
```
Mocha (B. Afena Cobham)
```
====================================
```

PARTY LINE MADNESS:
1-800 BLACK GENOCIDE

In my hood I'm probably the quietest one,
but on the Party Line Madness I'm so and so,
I'm this one, I'm a lonely ass Atilla the Hun.

"F--k you bitch", "I'll smack you hoe", "You
can eat a di-k and your mama too". The crime
of Black Genocide is what my people are calling
The Roach to do.

From New York to Cally -- Oh no! Not the east
coast, west coast game -- I can't help from
feeling the white man put this Party Line Madness
in my community to tighten that slave mentality
reign.

Using pre-paid numbers, stolen credit cards and
three-way conference with pride. If I can't do
it this way I'll find another way to dial
1-800 Black Genocide.

Telepersonal, Telecafe and the 8 Ball are all
the same. Another lethal injection into black
people's low self-esteem vein.

"It's just entertainment" -- "Well I call
here 'cause I'm bored", but no REAL black woman
should ever tolerate being labeled a whore.

1-800 Black Genocide, I hurt for other Party Line
dwellers -- folks with the lineage of African Kings
and Queens -- talking like they were born and raised
in jail house cellars.

1-800 Black Genocide a low budget addiction I must
kick. This Party Line Madness could never define me
'cause I'm on some true cipher sh--.

*She received her
Bachelor of Arts
degree in
Communications
(Radio/TV/Film) from
Marist College. Mocha
is currently the
Assistant to the
Director of Housing/
Resident Director at
Western Connecticut
State University. She
has served as Co-
founder/advisor to the
National Residence
Hall Honorary, Gino J.
Arconti Chapter and is
the current advisor to
the Black Student
Alliance. She is a
member of the
University Accreditation
Committee for Minority
Recruitment and
Retention. She is an
active member in Delta
Sigma Theta Sorority,
Incorporated, and the
Order of Eastern Star.*

==
Mocha (B. Afena Cobham)
==

Black Frame of Reference

Say it LOUD, I'm BLACK and I'm proud, but why does that seem to be an issue with those representing the majority crowd?

It's taken me a long time to develop a mindset with a BLACK frame of reference, Submerged in Afrocentric roots and I'm not pressed for anyone to understand this.

Caramel, Chocolate, Fudge, Butterscotch, BLACK Cherry, Cinnamon and Mocha makes it complete, those flavors cover the concept of BLACK, so don't get it twisted baby, 'cause ya know its sweet.

Colored, Negro, Nubian, Asiatic, and African American all equal the word BLACK, our name has gone through transformation, yet 500 years later we're still being attacked.

Brown, Mahogany, tan, bronze, red-bone, and chestnut; sprang from the roots of the color BLACK, attempting to pit one against the other is absurd or ebonically speaking "straight up whack".

It's taken me a long time to develop a mindset with a BLACK frame of reference, Submerged in Afrocentric roots and I'm not pressed for anyone to understand this.

I'm BLACK when I close my eyes for bed, I'm BLACK when I wake up and that's not something I will ever dread. I'm BLACK when I'm smiling and I'm BLACK when I'm pissed, I know a lot of folks who could never drop cipher like this. I'm BLACK, she's BLACK, he's BLACK, we're BLACK.

For those who can't handle that, I suggest you step the hell back. 'Cause see, It's taken me a long time to develop a mindset with a BLACK frame of reference, submerged in Afrocentric roots and I'm not pressed for anyone to understand this.

> *Mocha is also a published poet, Founder/ CEO of Mochalicious Entertainment and hopes to pursue a doctorate degree in Afro-American studies in the fall.*

Phaedra Davis

LOVELESS AND FEARLESS

times can be
uncontrollably
hard.
i find it
easy
to
lose
my SELF
in the
distance.
even though
things are
certain
but rare
in form,
which brings
guidance in souls.
REST EASY
as the wind
heals my pain.
by heavenly
sealing my wounds.

LOVE CAN TAKE TIME
LOVE CAN RUSH EASY.

its piercings leave
unattended
molds.

listen to the sound,
the wind of love.
as I CRADLE myself
in knowing, that
LOVE
could only
get EASIER.

PHAEDRA DAVIS

"When I am overwhelmed with silence, I find comfort with pen and a blank sheet of paper."

MY GAME HAS CHANGED

My game has changed...
My addiction came, sought out to be common.
Transformations,
gestures
hidden
beneath the surface.
Only few knew the truth.
My integrity,
had none.
I wasn't whole
nor was I pure.
Unadulterated,
spineless motivations.
With grips of ill mannered
ways
of seeing and relating
to those who loved me.
Who said they loved me.
Penny earned is a
penny LOST.
What is the rate on how
you relate
to your woman?
Good enough to be your wife
or do I embody,
the body
of the lust you crave?
To feed your insecurities of what
A REAL MAN should or could
be like.
Tasting and loving
1
2
or maybe 3.
I was at home.
I was neglected
I was denied.

I was TAUGHT,
to become a part
of your world.
To seek and see knowledge,
narrowly.
To give and feel love,
selfishly,
To use to rise above,
upwardly.
To deceive
to retain love,
with no boundaries.
Don't ponder for I no
longer am accustomed
to your world.
nor your ways.
Self love is bestowed
upon me.
Objectively,
I learned to
seek knowledge,
openly.
To give love,
unconditionally.
With love,
there are many
boundaries.
I SMILE AGAIN.
I no longer
am in need of your attention,
nor do I subject myself to your
ethics and the ways
on how you deal and misdeal
with the dilemmas of
your chaotic WORLD.

Rene L. Davis

RENE L. DAVIS

Rene was born in Washington, DC, but was raised in Northern Virginia by her mother, Lorraine, with her two younger sisters, Tammy and Abosede. She enjoys a well-balanced and fulfilling life with her three beautiful children, Eboni, James, and Justin.

Loving Me for Me

Yes, I've just turned Thirty!
And I'm proud of Me and what I've achieved.
I have beautiful children; all three uniquely made from Me!
I have a nice home, dependable car, and a career, you see!
Yes, I'm proud of Me and what I've achieved.

Some would say: being a good mother to my children;
Raising them with good values; and loving them compassionately,
Makes Me complete.

Some would say: that great performance at the office;
coming home to be the teacher; the cook, the housekeeper,
the nurse, the entertainer, the disciplinarian, mechanic, chauffeur,
referee, handyman, trash-man, mailman, psychoanalyst,
mind-reader, and all around problem solver,
Should be all I need to be.

How wrong could they be?
I've discovered Me, Yes the real Me!
I've learned that I can be anything and everything that
I want Me to be!

My Daddy and My Father told Me this;
There's nothing standing in front of Me, but Me!
This I know now, because God, his Son, and the Holy Spirit
Is not only by my side, but inside of Me.

Through all of my struggles and strife,
I've known that the army of determination,
The troops of faith and hope, and
The Holy Spirit of my Lord and Savior, Jesus Christ,
My Number One Warrior, surrounds Me.
They walk with Me and fight with Me in this war of
Challenges, pain, and suffering.
Together, and together only, on one accord,
We rise above defeat, casting down all fears, weaknesses and doubts.

However, I must first know and love Who I AM!
I must love Me and believe in Me to realize that I must
Win this battle and overcome these challenges.
Also, I must be willing to meet them and face them head on;
With pride, confidence and dignity.

Is this inside of Me?
How can it be?
How can this be when I've occasionally been weary,
Weak, sad and in despair?
Where was this strength, pride, and unspeakable power?

It was there all the time!
There, waiting for another tomorrow for Me to look into the mirror and see.
Seeking the truth of who I am and what's inside of Me.

I've learned that there's more to Me than said previously.
There's more to Me than just what people see.
I am the multi-faceted, multi-talented, multi-dimensional Me!

I love the smell of grass and roses, you see.
My heart melts at the sunrise and pounds deeply at the music's melody.
Reading inspirational pieces and giving birth to my own poetry soothes Me,
While, lying quietly listening to the rain tantalizes all the senses in Me.
Romantic, passionate and sensual; Yes, all describe the Woman you see.
Laughter, tears, and smiles full of joy, I indulge ever so freely.

While strategically planning my milestones in life,
I listen for what God has put Me here to be.
And as He sketches my life's agenda,
with structure and prayer I must proceed.
For it is His success that I must achieve.

Incorporating balance and focus in a fulfilled life, is what I aspire for Me;
Complete with love, romance, fun and a peaceful serenity.

For my hair, my skin, my flesh,
Thank you Lord, for what you've given Me.

For my mind, body, soul and spirit,
Thank you Lord, for what you've given Me.

For my health, my peace, and my time alone,
Thank you Lord, for what you've given Me.

For my memories, my experiences, my trials, tribulations and lessons,
Thank you Lord, for what you've given Me.

For my loved ones, my friends and my enemies too,
Thank you Lord, for what you've given Me.

For my wisdom, my courage, my faith and belief,
Thank you Lord, for what you've given Me.

For my strength, perseverance, tenacity and endurance,
Thank you Lord, for what you've given Me.

For the character of a real Woman, loyal, strong, compassionate and warm,
Thank you Lord, for what you've given Me.

Indeed, for the elegant Lady that you've raised Me to be.
Thank you Lord, for what you've given Me.

It has taken Me to see all of what other people see,
To see the Me that God has meant for Me to be.
Thank you Lord, for what you've given Me.

As I love Christ, for my gift of life,
I love Me for Me!

==
Rene L. Davis
==

Somebody tell me how. . .

When you love somebody
when you really, really love somebody
your heart and soul are in control
but there's no driver
there are no brakes
and sometimes there are no directions to unfold
Somebody tell me how
Please tell me how, because I just don't know

Feeling pain from a lost love
leaves you confused and beaten
disoriented and displaced
you want to breathe, but you forget how
you want to eat, but you're not hungry
you want to sleep, but you're restless
and you want to sit, but you pace
Somebody tell me how
Please tell me how, because I just don't know

You cry and you cry
your throat is sore and your eyes sting
that's not all and that's not it
deeply you cry, deep from your soul
deeply you hurt, and ache from your bones
you've never, ever pained like this
And you say
Somebody tell me how
Please tell me how, because I just don't know

Her professional career is in the government acquisitions industry. However, her real work is in the area of private therapeutic foster care services. I contribute an awesome amount of love and time reaching out to nurture special teenagers and revitalize the essential hope elements in their lives.

Reflections of joyous occasions and happy moments
invade the peace in your mind
once again you smile as you flip through your memories
you laugh, loud and hearty with passion and
then suddenly, you're alone
all alone and your voice is the only voice you hear
your laugh becomes empty and pretentious
your smile is overcome by gloom and sadness
reality sits beside you, while today's pain knocks at your door
you don't want to open it and you don't have to,

because today's pain has a key
then you digress into tears
and say
Somebody tell me how
Please tell me how, because I just don't know

I don't know how to go on
how to pick up from here and go over there
where there was joy and laughter to move me
there's now pain and agony that keeps hurting me
I don't want to be here anymore
I want what I used to have and used to be
But it doesn't want me anymore
Go your own way now, he says
I know you're hungry and I have
but I choose not to give you anymore
But please, I say,
I'm suffering and I need it to breathe
I need it to feel,
I need it to think
I need it to awaken in the morning
I need it to sleep at night
I need you and I need the love you gave me
that fulfilled me with overwhelming joy
that placed the beautiful and confident smile on my face
that became oxygen to me
that poured into my empty trinket that I now call a soul
Somebody tell me how
Please tell me how, because I just don't know

The passion that used to fulfill me
I drowned in it deeply
I depended on it like my heartbeat
The lovemaking that piloted me into the heavens
The oneness and closeness of our flesh, unavoidably compelling
this is ecstasy
that was ecstasy
and now it's gone, it's all gone
like leaves in the winter time
voided, cold and unfeeling
Somebody tell me how

Please tell me how, because I just don't know

======================================
Tracy Evans
======================================

"God Bless The Child"
    (to L.O.M.)

God bless the child who's haunted by ghosts...
Running away from home won't run you away from self.
Child, this world ain't been perfect
since the picking of the forbidden,
as I'm sure you already know.
But people do love you--you've got a whole family--
even though they aren't all blood, and God above you,
below you, around you, within you...
What's gotten into you?
Turning people's souls inside out.
You haven't got a clue as to what this ol' evil world will do to you.
And yet you're running for it with open arms,
While others
wait and watch and pray and grieve
and hope and yearn and still believe
that you'll come home and things will get better.
Because without you
your mother has lost a daughter;
your brother, a sister
your auntie, a niece
and Snow, even Snow must miss ya.
And who will I leave to get grapes for?--
But return only with oranges, apples, Chick-Fil-A fries
and herb-fortified juices because there were no grapes?
And, who will tell me that they don't want the juice
because they like grapes but not the juice that tastes like grapes?
All those roles-
daughter, sister, niece, dog torturer and grape seeker
can only be filled by you.
So we're waiting for you to come home.
Nights ago, I came in your room to make sure that
you weren't too hot or too cold
and to hear you breathe.
But now I hope that you aren't breathing too hard

TRACY EVANS

Tracy is a 24-year old artist and revolutionary from Queens, New York. She currently resides in Atlanta, Georgia, where she received her Bachelor of Arts degree in African-American Studies from Emory University.

110

from all that running
From Yourself.
So if you come back,
I promise that you can be whoever you are
and I still won't think you're crazy.
And you can write how you'd like
and you can talk with your tongue
and sometimes, I'll even let you slide on your patience
But I won't let you suck your thumb.
And I won't tell your 12-year old mind
lies about vinegar killing the already planted sperm
or throw your poems away
and we can draw all types of flowers
in the color lime-green and build your self-esteem.
Because that's really the problem...
or so it seems...
God bless the child who's haunted by ghosts.

UNTITLED

I know all too well

that tears fall

out the sides

of your eyes

when you lie

on your back

and down the sides

of your nose

when you're sitting up

I even know

that tears may escape you

when your eyes are closed

because I tried to hold them back once

on the J

and the Muslim brother standing

over me said,

SISTERAREYOUALRIGHT?

Stephanie Griswold-Ezekoye

THE TROUBLED HEART

I looked into your eyes
   And saw a troubled man
Love starved and hungry
   For a gentle hand
Wanting to trust
   In what you hear and see
Yet time has taught you
   That this can't possibly be.

I looked into your eyes
   And saw sparkles of gold
Surrounding deep brown ovals
   That reached into my soul
I trembled from the emotion
   That swelled deep within
But couldn't speak my heart's true thoughts
   Because of where I am.

I looked into your eyes
   And realized instantly,
That the years of your confinement
   Had smothered what comes free.
That to live in such conditions
   Must create an impenetrable wall,
Which blocks the inside feelings
   And repels the sight of all.

I believe you have a pure heart,
   And wisdom beyond your years.
And love overflowing its physical bounds
   With a spirit that reflects your tears.
I believe you know the righteousness,
   Which exists in every man;
And you follow your spirits beliefs,
   In any way you can.
It's time you bring together
   The lessons of your spiritual trials,

STEPHANIE GRISWOLD-EZEKOYE

Stephanie has been an author, private designer and training consultant in the fields of Human Resource Development, Cultural Diversity, Management, and Substance Abuse since 1978. She is author of Who Am I? A Comprehensive Personal Growth and Development Program.

She has been the Executive Director for the Addison Terrace Learning Center, a multicultural substance abuse prevention, intervention and treatment agency since 1982.

So that healing, loving, trusting and giving
　　　　Become a part of your life's miles.

From her book "FROM BEGINNING TO BEGINNING:
A POETIC JOURNEY THROUGH LIFE".

======================================

Stephanie Griswold-Ezekoye

======================================

ARE YOU A LITTLE WOMAN MAN?

Are you a little woman man
　　　　Dreaming of the time
When you find that "Little Woman"
You can hold and mold in the middle of your hand?

Are you a little woman man
　　　　Searching the world for that petite fit
That snugs just right in the middle of the night....
That you can hold and mold in the middle of you hand?
　　　　Are you a little woman man?

Or maybe.....
You'd like to feel what you hold
Those smooth round curves of a healthy woman.
Maybe....
You'd like to be held softly and tightly
　　　　With the firm, tender caress of the big woman
Whose love envelopes you and says, MMMMMM,
　　　　Baby, that's so sweet.
A big woman who molds and holds and....
Slowly feels you right where you need to be?

Have you become a big woman man now?
　　　　Have you become an any woman man now?
Have you become a love me right woman man now?
Have you become a big/little, tall/short, fat/skinny
　　　　JUST LOVE ME RIGHT MAN NOW?

From her book "FROM BEGINNING TO BEGINNING:
A POETIC JOURNEY THROUGH LIFE".

L. K. ROSE FORD

Rose was born and raised in Atlanta, Georgia. She and her husband, Alfred, have been married for 29 years. She loves writing, family gatherings, and dancing. She has written several short stories, children's books, and a novel. She has given readings of her book at various elementary schools.

=====================================
L. K. "Rose" Ford
=====================================

The woman that had you

She's not the mama of Hallmark fame,
She was never called that, She was called by her name.
She couldn't take you to "Six-Flags", Or "Disneyworld",
She was too tired to ride on things that "Twirl".
She never bought you a "cap gun', Or any ' war-toy',
She tried to make a gentleman, of her little boy.
She was never aggressive, She didn't know how to fight,
Yet she chased those boys off-you, with the shotgun that night.

She hasn't slept a whole night in the last twenty years,
She sat praying over you, and telling God her fears.
When you graduated from high-school, she cried with joy,
She was so proud of her little boy, She was still,
young and pretty, with a figure so 'fine,'
But, she said, "I can't put no man over this child of mine."
She worked in fast-food places, and hotels and bars,
So you could attend that 'College of the stars'.
She sat at your bedside for every sick day,
The woman that had you, couldn't pull herself away.
When your girlfriend got pregnant, and you weren't wed,
She screamed and she cried, and she shook her head.
Yet, she drove her to the clinic every time, She said,
"I got to watch over this child of mine."
When your girl was in labor, she sat patiently there,
waiting, praying, pulling her hair.
She was so proud, and thanked God for her world,
when she saw her grandbaby, a beautiful girl.

When you got your degree, She was surprised, with a tear in her eye,
when you thanked everybody, but her you passed by.
She tried to give you your gift, but you hurried away,
"Annie, I'm going out," you said. "You don't have to stay."
She wasn't mad at you, After all, It was your day.
When you got married in Cleveland so far away,
She shrugged and said, "It is their day."
When you stopped coming around, Because you hated her street,
She remembered walking down it with you to your 'swim meet'.
When you moved to your home, on the north side of town,
Your wife let you know, she didn't want her around.
She said "She talks so' country, and she isn't polite",
"And she doesn't fit in, with our friends that are white"
You told her "We're busy, Don't visit so much,
Now you shy away from her hug or touch,
When she started coughing, as you got your award,
You asked her to leave, and it broke her heart.
She cried all the way home, for the rest of the day,
When she wasn't crying, she fell on her knees to pray.
She sank lower, and lower, you rose higher than high.
You were enjoying your life, She was praying to die.
The lord was with her, But she's not the same.
The woman that had you, Is a homeless woman named MAME.

(from "life ain't nothing but a series of words." Book II)

=======================================
L. K. "Rose" Ford
=======================================

Lye soap and "Conglomeration soup"

Ms. Greeley's making "soup" again,
lye soaps on Thursday night
They say that both are best when made
by "coal-oil" and lanterns light.
Ms. Watkins down the street, with her "gossipy" little group,
they all get together and make Conglomeration soup.

My home's in Atlanta, Georgia,
I'm a girl that's growing fast.
I'll be the next to learn the ladies' secrets,
so that their traditions can last.

They say I have to know it, they say I don't have a choice.
the seventh daughter, of the seventh daughter,
must give the group a voice.

She must learn to count,
She must learn to write,
She must learn to read the book.
The book that tells her when and why,
both the soup and soap to cook.

I went to sleep, and woke up again,
I thought I heard a scream.
I told the grown-ups about it,
they said it was only a dream.

I thought I saw the Greeleys here,
talking to the ladies' group. Ms. Watkins said,
Mr. Greeley, should have his head put in a "loop."
I woke up the next morning, to the smell of lye, and lime.
Ms. Watkins' flowers seem so pretty,
every year around this time.

They say Mr. Greeley "ran-off" last night,
with a girl about sixteen, every year around this time,
some mean man does it seems.

Mr. Greeley used to come home "liquored-up,"
and on Ms. Greeley he would pounce.
I heard her tell Ms. Angie Sellers,
She would pay, sixteen cents an ounce.

Ms. Angie said, "Girl, I heard that!"
"Let me know I'll tell the group."
"Chile our children need to eat,
 some good 'Conglomeration "soup."

A ladies' group with their same name,
has met since slavery time, They make soap,

and "special 'soup, and for dill pickles,
they make "brine."

The ladies grow the prettiest flowers,
using "animal fat", and lime.
This group stayed young, and "wrinkle-free,"
No matter what hardships they went through.
While "Old master" dried up at 37, face
'looked like a leather shoe.'

But, back to Mr. Greeley, for I digress, it seems.
Mr. Greeley and his young girl, barely past the age sixteen.
They say he left last Friday night, after he burst in on the ladies' group.
Saturday morning, all their children ate, "Conglomeration soup."

Mr. Watkins in the hospital, I heard he got a scald,
Right in the top of his head, where he's started going bald.

Ms. Watkins threw out a pot of soup.
Said it didn't match her "flair." I walked by just then.
"Is that soup full of hair?"

Anyway, Ms. Angie's calling me. She wants me to peel potatoes,
and not throw away the "skins." "Lye soap needs potato peels,
it seems, to keep the grease from settling in."

(from "life ain't nothing but a series of words." Book II)

==================================
Craig Gill
==================================

Untitled

Finally, a day off
Well, not really.
I shoulda been elsewhere,
Isn't that silly?

Guess you know my routine,
How she makes me change my mind.
But damn, when we're together,
We're suspended in time.

By the way, TIME, what's your problem?
Can't you see we're not done yet?
But I don't think it heard me,
On that I can bet.

I was headed in another direction,
My pager went off, no need for discretion.
I knew it was, well, "You-know-who",
Her message said simply, "I LOVE YOU".

I was back where I started,
Rushed home in a hurry.
She'll be here soon,
No need to worry.

That's the part that gets me,
She's like my soul mate.
She took me back to the place,
Where we had our first date.

Hours are like minutes,
I know you've heard that before.
But I'm telling you the truth,
She had just walked through the door.

What's the deal with a day off?
How long does it last?
If I was where I shoulda been,
It would have NEVER ended this fast.....

====================================
Craig Gill
====================================

Untitled

i sit in awe
as i watch you walk
across the room
with every graceful step
your body displays power
and commands respect.
not just because of your beauty
because you are the mother of
our civilization
A PROUD BLACK WOMAN!

the sweet melody of your words
gently caresses the air around me,
my heart is set ablaze.
i wonder how any man can resist being
mesmerized by your beauty and inner spirit.
i can't!

the sincerity of your smile is like the
morning's first ray's of light
bursting over the horizon
feeling me with inner peace and reassurance
that somehow...some way...
everything will be all right.

i can't help but to think...
you are my future.

```
==================================
```
Shawn Goins
```
==================================
```

SHAWN GOINS

Shawn resides in Chicago, Illinois, with his 3-year old son, Ashante, whom he loves very much. He is a test engineer and writes test programs. Shawn has been writing since he was 8 years old.

"I write poetry because it helps me get a lot of things out of my mind that may be either bothering me or something that I think about...."-

THE GREETING

I observe you walking toward me
As far as my eyes can see
Could it be you're my enemy
Who's trying to get to me

Could it be that you're that brother
Who wants to shake my hand because
you understand the plan
We have to uncover to get along with one another

Steadily we approach

As we get near, in my heart there is no fear
For I sense our souls becoming the same
We travel down the same road, society has taken the same toll
On our race; we pick up the pace, soon we'll be face-to- face

We are face-to-face

We acknowledge one another with a nod
As soon as our eyes meet, we speak to greet each other
You are my brother

Shawn Goins

Adversary

For all I do, I still can't do right by you
I go to school to educate myself for a better future
You call me stupid, unintelligent, and uneducated
Racist
I have an honest job to support myself and my family
You call me a drug dealer because I can afford nice things
Police
I help my brothers improve themselves to become better people
You say I'm a killer and have no regard for black life
Media
I work hard to try to make a good life for myself
You're to busy back stabbing me because you're envious and jealous
Black men
I go to the store to buy groceries
You call me a thief and watch every move I make
Bigot
I wear my clothes different than what the public says is correct
You call me a thug, gangbanger, or hoodlum
Society
I am a young black male full of potential and dreams
You call me a young black male who's destined for jail or death
Statistics
I am a man who loves and takes care of my kids
You call me a deadbeat dad who
runs away from his responsibilities
Judicial system
I am a man who loves, respects, and honors
 black women
You call me a bum, a dog, and constantly say
there are no good black men
Black women
As positive as I am, your negativity is
weighing me down
You always try to demean me and shy away
 from my good qualities
Who is my adversary?
You tell me

> *"...All of the poems I write are about me in one way or another. "*
>
> Shawn often volunteers his time working in the community with children, and says that he loves everything about his brothers and sisters (the good and the bad). His motto is, Nothing but love.

====================================
Christopher Hare
====================================

The Beast Within

What times are these
that spawn such things,
from the deep dark depths
comes the Beast Within?

He asks not for permission
nor gives a reason why,
his desires are satisfied
within a blink of an eye.

To tame it is a challenge
many have tried, so the story is told,
its lust knows not of age
and craves both young and old.

One side is good,
the other side bad,
one boasts of love,
the other of the women he has had.

Without each other
neither will survive,
for personal satisfaction
both must separately strive.

They care not for others
in their quest for heated passion,
so, guard close your womanly purity
or to you, this will happen.

CHRISTOPHER HARE

Christopher a/k/a Valentino, the Poetic Joker, resides in Woodbridge, VA, with his wife, son and daughter. He was in the Marines for 9 fun-filled years, where interests in writing poetry became more apparent.

"It allowed me to express myself, or any bottled emotions I was experiencing at any given time. I patterned my writing style in a manner that could be used by anyone in everyday conversation to let their feelings be known or to simply allow them to escape to a place of seclusion."

======================================
Christopher Hare
======================================

The Lonely Diva

High in tower
with a view of the land
the Diva waits patiently
for her Prince Charming's hand.

Desired by all men
though alone she sleeps
erotic dreams are her escape,
when awakened, she clutches her pillow and weeps.

To confine her passion
is nothing less than a sin,
but when unleashed without control
she possesses the drive of ten.

Through rage for the time she's lost
and her restraints now broken
she uses her body thoughtlessly,
as man's undeserved love token.

With little self-worth
and a heart just as cold
she feels like nothing more,
than a piece of meat to be bought or sold.

A Diva's world is empty
with no one to call her own,
she would rather end her reign
than sit on a hollow thrown.

.....Christopher took the name Valentino because of his long eyelashes, women told him that he looked like he wore mascara like Rudolph Valentino. He added on Poetic Joker to complete his identity as a lover of poetry and an underpaid comedic sidekick.

" I attribute my claim to fame to be my sense of humor and my ability to see a lighter side in any situation."

SUSAN HARRIGAN

Susan is an educator, and currently a dance teacher at an elementary school in the Bronx, New York City. She enjoys taking dance classes (African and Salsa at the moment) and practicing T'ai C'hi.

" I have been known to burst into poetic inspiration. Since she joined the internet community a little over a year ago, she's come across some exciting places, like the Poets Niche, that give opportunities for poets to share those trains of thought....."

====================================

Susan Harrigan

====================================

Mixed Emotions

I wept when I read them
your words pierced so deep
left speechless in emotion

How happy I was to see you
real and vibrant
knowing it was you
and glimpsing part of you on the inside

No greater gifts given
than to share the depth of your mind
inner hopes, hates and hunches
the treasures you bring to us on the outside

I must admit I warmed to you
inviting you to enter my mind and explore
it was the most intimate thing I could give you
for what it's worth
I respect you more

In the softness I was saddened
wished hard for the dreams
not to take hold
too open in my contentment
feeling the fool for sharing my soul

In moments, a hug and good-byes
assurance that all was fine
parting in opposite directions
separate destinations
I found you beautiful

I used to dream of you through your voice
You were always on the edge of my sight
you flowed through my mind in the day
and I called your presence to me at night

You will live and love another
Love given
unreturned

learning what will be
with faith in my heart
seeking peace
I journey

==================================
Susan Harrigan
==================================

Vision

Each of us is in the midst of his own rolling tide
Struggling for each breath to keep us alive
I see the flowers grow where none should be like
the child born of a rape placed in a loving family
The cloud in the sky changes colors and hues
and when darkened with rain seem to reflect the
pain of the victims of family abuse
but I know from the past that cycles must turn
And in seeing simple beauty the lesson I've learned
is not to let life's injustices seal my fate
to fight the poisons piled high on life's plate
to seek in the madness the love that shines through
and when you struggle with your poisons
these gifts I offer to you

If I reach out my hand
would you reach back for me?

".....Here's a little trivia about me: I REALLY LOVE the Warner Bros. Cartoons (Bugs Bunny and the Loony Tunes/Merrie Melodies Gang). I wonder when they are going to put The Electric Company back on PBS Stations for children and BARNEY HAS NOTHING ON THE SESAME STREET CREW!!! GO ERNIE!! "

I dreamed of the beach and you with me...
and I heard your voice say,
"How can you ponder small wonders
when we're enveloped by pain?
We're always on the losing side
when we have the most to gain.
Sweet small things don't help us when we disagree,
and to this day, you know you don't understand
the frustrations in me."
I looked ahead of us as I fell silent in wonder and awe...
In front of us, in Jamaica, rushed Dunns River Falls
confused and annoyed, you asked me what I saw

"I see the macro and the microcosms of life...
the caress and the cascade, the crash and the creation.
I see the swell of suffocation and the breath of life."
The mystery of time, fast, slow, and never waiting..
I see the deep and the shallow, the tears and the blood, the womb
and the waste, the clarity and cloudiness of the Eternal...

"I love interesting and wholesome conversation and learning about the cultural and spiritual side of people. I hope, as you read the selections in this compilation, you enjoy the insights of the poets and confirm the wonder of the mind in words."

=================================

Nadeen Herring

=================================

SON

Never so fulfilled
At a time
In my life when
Misery was my company
    and fear was my mate---

To you I owe my life
Harmonious at long last
After weathering so many storms
Never do you need worry
Kindred spirit
    for
You are
Outranked only by God
    and together we will build
        the
Utopia of our *soulstice*.

NADEEN HERRING

Nadeen was born in the Bronx in New York City. She spent most of her life in Harrisburg, Pennsylvania, but now resides in Atlanta, Georgia. Nadeen is a proud black sister, daughter, mother, wife, teacher, friend, leader and follower. She is currently teaching high school English at a local international school.

Writing has always been her first love, and only recently has she considered using pen and paper as the weapon of choice in terms of personal independence and as a means of creating an altering voice within an anti-social society.

===
Nadeen Herring
===

Good Natured

If my nature could
divide
the Moon into one
thousand quarters
Would you eat each piece
as if it were your last
From the tips of my fingers
Sticking
and
Licking

Good?

And if the Moon
divide
could to my nature
quarter thousands
Could you piece the last
and eat

Good?

The Moon to my Nature
to the Nature
 to Nature
  so natural
So we
  We to thee
Nature

Is our Calling.

I see it this eve ---
Quarters of you
And me
For the whole

Good.

Nadeen's goals include finishing her doctorate, co-authoring a book on Latino/African-American relationships and schooling, finishing a book of poetry, and establishing a school that caters to the spiritual, social, and academic needs of children of color. She considers it divine-intervention that she was chosen to share herself with others (she always wanted to be a journalist, not a teacher) and even a bigger blessing to learn from a sometimes forgotten generation. She believes in the miracle of self-preservation, the necessity of the spirit, and the sanctity of family.

"Without such acknowledgments, I am empty."

===
Akilah Holyfield
===

The Eye Dance

I love to play the eye dance
it's like a slight split
second blink of
eye contact.
You feel the gaze,
but when you look
they...
look away.
Only for that slight, split
second blink of
eye contact
you positively feel
THE VIBES.
I look.
You Look...
You dance.
You look.
I look...
I dance
Until...
We dance together.

AKILAH HOLYFIELD

Akilah currently resides in Atlanta, and is a psychology student at Georgia State University. She has been very active in the creative world. She has performed in the National Black Arts Festival and written two books.

===
Akilah Holyfield
===

NIGHT

At night when every one is fast asleep,
And the house is quiet except for the stairs that creak.
Little people walk around,
Very busy without a sound
They push people out their beds,
And put little thoughts in your heads.
You may never even know they're there,
Cause they might be hiding in your hair.
But they are here every night,
And they leave when it gets light.

=====================================
Sharyn P. Hunter
=====================================

First

Ever notice the wonders of joy
Ever feel the rapture of delight
I am my mother's child
She has given me flight.

As I sit here on the balcony
Watching this sunrise
I can see me in my mother
I can hear her thoughts devise

You will take over now
Take us, depart
Egypt, Senegal, Ethiopia, Dakar
Carry us with you in your heart!

=====================================
Sharyn P. Hunter
=====================================

Descendants

As I look into the mirror
Faces of the past I see
Kathryn, Richard, Lucy, Mary
And then, Emily?
No, that's ME!

Windows open in my mind
Visions sneak in at every turn
Reuben, Calvin, Charlotte, Horace
Oh, their struggles I have learned

Melungeon, Black, Octoroon, Mulatto
And White on more than occasion
Than they want
Us to be

And here generations later
We're not slaves, we're free
And they're the MINORITY!

SHARYN P. HUNTER

Sharyn was born in South Bend, Indiana, but calls Columbia, Maryland home. She is married with three daughters, one son and 6.5 grandchildren. She taught in the DC Public School System for 26 years. Sharyn attended Howard University, is a member of the Alpha Kappa Alpha Sorority, and Mt. Pisgah AME Church.

Her hobbies include writing, crafts, interior decorating, and traveling. Sharyn's passion, however, is genealogy. She is currently writing a genealogical article about her great great grandfather for the Middle Tennessee Genealogical Society. Her accomplishments include researching, finding and purchasing an early 1800's replica of a chair made by her great great grandfather. She has also completed her first children's book entitled Where Jamal Sleeps.

===================================

Saleem Abdal-Khaaliq

===================================

SALEEM ABDAL-KHAALIQ

"Writing is a form of pantheism for me, a continuum of opposites that are always evolving. It is liberating yet confining, it is peaceful while being chaotic; it is clarity mixed with confusion and it is a healing within a contagion. All vying for a piece of the paper at the same time."

? Correction Fluid

The day brings paragraphs
to her fingertips.
Clean white sheets between rollers   ... the bed
remains unmade.

Her margins set by others.
Mind numbed by-lines that permit her
to hold down the DELETE key, long enough   ... to inscribe another's
choosing.

The millennia began at these keys,
pounding out the meaning of her inner being.
Yet, the turn of the century turned out to be   ... one less writer
sitting by the keyboard.

    INSERT __ stop __ COLON

Restless digits fumble to unlock
a frenzy of correctness.
Punctuated, ribbonless etchings in black & white   ... often read by lips
late into the night.

Grief, in C-a-p-i-t-a-l letters
frames her work station.

Mouthing the musings of an utter fool   ... on Monogrammed stationery

She hits RETURN to jump start a life
and BACK SPACE to a time in
her now inked-dried PERIOD   ... among the hidden words she rights

    COMMA __ stop __ SEMI-COLON

a Parent (in parentheses) on carbon-less paper.
This pathetic actress who slams the SPACE BAR
for another drink   ... to drown the old silence, in a new way
(loudly)

then fast-forwards to her next role --
pressing hard against the SHIFT-LOCK
yet, remains totally out of CONTROL   ... only the fantasies have
become
indelible

She knows the ribbon in the sky
spells destiny without her.
An index finger away from writing her life   ... without Magic
Marker

She PAGES DOWN quickly, as if
she can ESCAPE her Life-Sentence --
              by wanting to be   who she isn't
(?)

```
=====================================
```
Saleem Abdal-Khaaliq
```
=====================================
```

THE SIXTH GENERATION CHILD

I am of the 4th Dimension
where questions answer themselves
and problems are the solution.

A 6th Generation Child -- knowledgeable,
where rivers flow uphill like
the Nile:
        Past bygone slavery & bestiality.

I am Appalachian high & Sahara dry,
a Universal Child of an unseen era
from the unforetold future
of a misplaced and forgotten Age.

I am the 6 Wonders of the World,
my Son the 7th & last
                         Everlasting.

Beware this 6th Generation Child
my prophetic progeny
shall be the Master of Fate.
The Firegodcreator of an end
                         to Beginning again.

"...How anything I write is ever understood, I have no idea. It is hell orbiting an oasis. It is the other side of never, the very bottom of the abyss and the apex of the Mount all wrapped into one.

Truly, of all that I have experienced and witnessed in this sojourn on earth, the highest compliment that I could ever receive would be that of 'above all else he was a Poet'."

GHADA EL KURD -
Ghada was born in
Doha, Qatar, and
currently resides in
Amman of the Hashimite
Kingdom of Jordan. She
was educated in Jordan's
elite schools, and
received her Bachelor of
Science in Business
Administration in 1998.

Ghada El Kurd

I remember

I remember,
I remember that night before you left,
I remember how I held you in my arms,
I remember holding your head close to my chest and near my heart,
I remember tears slipping down my face and into your hair,
I remember looking into your eyes,
I remember the joy in them,
I remember the pain in them,
I remember my thumb touching the corner of your eye,
I remember finding it wet,
I remember just how I felt,
I remember feeling gratitude for having you,
I remember the tears we both shed,
I remember....

I remember,
I remember early in the morning just before you went away,
I remember you walking through the door, sunlight trailing behind you,
I remember how you looked at me,
I remember those huge sad eyes,
I remember them piercing my own,
I remember your arms encircling me,
I remember them crushing me tenderly,
I remember my fingers reaching up to your face,
I remember them tracing down to your shoulder-blades,
I remember how we kissed and then forever held,
I remember standing at the iron gate,
I remember you smiling sadly,
I remember crying as you drove away,
I remember...

====================================
Ghada El Kurd
====================================

Reflecting

Ever since we were kids,
We were good friends.
We grew up together.
We did grow into each other.
That is for sure.
So why was I so insecure?
Think I was coy?
Well, so were you boy!
Reflecting on how it all started,
And how much they minded,
I can see where things went wrong.
And remember the silence loud and strong.
Yet, we managed to get around,
And choose our ground.
Let the whole world see,
How much I love thee.
I love thee.

Ghada is the Head Designer and manages a Fashion House, which she helped establish back in 1994. Ghada loves to read, write poetry, and is currently working on her first novel.

Ajani Kush

AJANI KUSH

*" I'm a Jamaican-born,
Brooklyn-raised, college-
educated woman who is
answering a call that has
been as consistent as
my heartbeat and as
persistent as my five-
year old.*

*Maasai, my beautiful
son, inspires me daily to
be better, do better and
create a better world for
him to grow up in."*

WHITE HEAT

The village is burning.
Can't you see the flames
licking their lips
waiting to claim our souls.

The village is burning.
But our drying well can only
spit drops of wet relief.
We didn't prepare
for the white heat
that strikes in the night.
Consuming our chafed
reeds of manhood
that lay unnourished
in the arid sun.

'bout time

Mr. Scott was still at home
on Moffat Street
among the cracked sidewalks
and crack houses.
Bushwick had been home
since 1945 when he and Margrit
married after the war --- before
the war zone moved
home to Brooklyn.
He was not about to be
uprooted by a bunch of Gapkids
boppin' through the billboards of life.
Besides, Margrit died
in this house so
why shouldn't he?
Tho' he wasn't sure why
it was taking so long.
After all he was 78
last spring!

One day Mr. Scott saw
Mrs. Ruiz being accosted
by members of the Mo' Fat crew
saying her son owed them
money for crack.
Mr. Scott told them cussingly
about the respect
of the good old days
and told them to retreat
"or else"!
This they didn't appreciate
'cause it wouldn't do to be
dissed on your own turf by
"some ol' ass punk".
So as the safety
clicked off the .45
Mr. Scott thought only of Margrit,
he smiled and sighed
"bout time".

======================================
Ajani Kush
======================================

Have Mercy (a sista's story)

Did I stutter
when I said no?
Did my shoves not correspond
with the feelings that I felt
that night
our date somehow went wrong.
What did I do to turn him on?
My cleavage was well kept.
My hair, my face weren't overdone.
My butt I kept in check.
He said he'd like to know me.
I took him at his word.
He said he'd like to love me, or
at least that's what I heard.
Putting on my sweetest smile,
I gently told him
after
we get to know our hearts
and we've experienced the
laughter
can we fall into each others' arms
and love.

His eyes turned old
he pushed me and I
hardly made a sound.
His arms like steel enclosed me
and this body hit the ground.

I floated over watching,
he overruled her pleas.
I couldn't stay within her
as he propped her on her knees.
Have mercy!

When I returned we cried a while
then gathered up the bits

of soul
of life
of dignity
all scattered from the hits.
It was over.
We were history,
gone from us all our dreams.
We once were one
but now we're none,
how could he stand the screams?

Yes, he got to know her
in a way I'd never tell.
Why bother, no one would believe,
it seems impossible to conceive:
The fact is she couldn't yell.
The pain was great but greater
was the shatter of my soul
as it burst into three pieces.
Never once again the whole.
One piece stayed inside her and
the other flew to God,
but the one
we simply can't dismiss.
In him each time he'll reminisce
"'bout the bitch that tried to front and dis'"?!
A smile, his lips will crown
as he carries me around
while they lay her in the ground
'cause we could not bear
the sound
of our soul
gagged and bound.
Please, mercy...

Being a writer, a self-proclaimed mouthpiece for her generation, is how she has chosen to make a difference. Over the years, self-expression has become the most important thing in Ajani's life.

*"Writing was the very first outlet for my true feelings to be heard. It all started in kindergarten when I wrote I hate Mommy on one of my books after being punished for some childhood infration. (Sorry Mom, you know I didn't mean it). It was through this self-expression that Ajani discovered the power of the written word. Those squiggles on paper made my feelings known, my teacher worried, my mom got upset and created a dialogue between the three of us to flush out the truth. I've never stopped writing since. Whether I'm sharing my own experiences or have been moved to be the voice for others, when I'm writing...
...I'm free!"*

==

Jaci LaMon

==

the breakup, chapter two

JACQUELINE LAMON

Jaci is a writer and teacher, residing in Southern California. Her poetry has appeared in various publications and she is a frequent contributor to the Poets Niche. Jaci, a graduate of Mount Holyoke College and UCLA School of Law, is currently completing a collection of poetry entitled, In The Arms Of One Who Loves Me.

asses shift
hands wringing hands
nails tapping surfaces worn with scars and grooves
breath heavy upon unbreathed breath
eyes lowered
empty dark and dripping
your lips moving
remembering lips and tongue and teeth and
hair
so shamed and so fulfilled
there is no other path around this piercing
we chat about the job and weather
speak once familiar dialects
of body language revisited
you scratch your head
releasing a memory embedded
behind the ear in which she last left whispers
and convulse involuntarily while you think
of the second hour taste
of the fingers on your right hand
LOOK AT ME
i am not going to make this easy for you
not going to pat your back
or shake that hand
give you a box lunch and carfare
not going to run the tape

WE CAN ALWAYS BE FRIENDS
WE CAN ALWAYS BE FRIENDS
WE CAN ALWAYS BE FRIENDS
i mean
just how many times
are you going to leave me
before i have been left
indeed...

====================================

Jaci LaMon

====================================

a woman's mood...

i look
but there is no semblance of you
no letters that entice
no voice which calls my name
no need to turn around

i come and go
wait for wind to disrupt my thoughts
i should vacuum
instead i fix coffee
let it grow cold

if i could dream
i would sleep another time
disrupting this void
if i could sing
i would climb upon a note
and croon you into now

the waiting is hard
the wanting
surreal

the where and how and why
unanswered
and nothing is getting done.

==
Jaci LaMon
==

three

you look at me
reaching touching
holding
but your hand does not reach for
my hand
your fingers do not caress my palms
or notice the arms that crave an embrace
for
i am no longer woman
no longer she who is beyond the tangible
just
three body parts
i no longer have need for honeyed face
or lotioned knee
or craving mind
for i am
just
three body parts
derriere
cleavage
and that place you call yours
to you
i am
the sum total of parts one two three
there is nothing else major comprising of me
my legs
you say
serve mighty purpose
to transport the three
to carry them swiftly to
wherever
you may be
yet
i am no longer woman
just three body parts
my left ear--
she once craved to hear you sing my name

shout out
and grip my shoulder twins strong
they are dying lonely now
neglected children that they are
and yes i remember
the days when i once
twisted your touches
in my hair
oh yes i remember
the days of yesterday
before the days of right way your way
when you loved my breath
before it left my soul's harbor
because it was mine
when three comprised
you
and me
and eternity
applauded by rain
supported by a cast of a thousand stars
not only the functional task to be
and body parts three

```
===================================
```
Dawn Landon
```
===================================
```

Dreams of Bob
(for my Jamaica 98 crew)
∧∧∧∧∧∧∧∧∧∧∧∧∧∧∧∧∧∧∧∧∧∧∧∧∧

sky teardrops wake me
            (you feel my emptiness)
no glimpse of sun to guide my way
            (I'll be home soon)

wheels spin closer to final destination
wind sighs through island trees
I hear you calling me
            I'm coming,
my heart answers your plea

listening to your words of love
            (anticipating our embrace)
they calm my frantic need
            (I see the house from here)
is that your shadow near the tree?

rushing through the doorway,
            (I call your name)
suddenly, our song begins
            (a muffled refrain)
bidding me, REMEMBER

though the love is real...
its all just been a dream

DAWN LANDON

Dawn was born and raised in Baltimore City, though she feels she was wronged since she has more of an affinity for Jamaica (hence her love for Bob Marley, dancehall, coco bread, and Ting). After graduating from high school, she joined the US Navy and Uncle Sam graciously allowed her to travel the world. After five years of government enslavement, she attended George Washington University in Washington, DC.

Reflecting on Love with Neff

I was talking with a friend today
--- about men
She's found an African Prince
Black Man in concrete jungle
We reflect on why she's not satisfied with him
--- frustration over petty social conventions

I remember who I believe to be my first love
--I think we're afraid
Of what?
--Being in love.
That uncontrollable feeling
in the barren pit of chests

       Who stole your heart?
       And left you with a space that
       no one, or nothing, can fill.

Being open to unexpected hurts
--Giving up that part so essential to the whole
giving me (you)
to he, who knows so little about you (me)

Later, I replay the conversation in my mind
What about L-0-V-E scares me?
Craving that which I so repel

If u feel   -

             -

      -

    nothing

     -

       -

        -

can hurt

Who hurt your heart,
and bruised it in a place that
no one, or nothing, can heal?

--Am I lonely?
Or tired of being alone?
--No matter, I comfort myself
        anger and pain remain locked inside,
        sparks of emotion revealed briefly

--Would love free me
                to be
(But am I)   me?

Without he to complete
I'm part of a whole that has yet to be
But I'm impatient
I wait for no one
                to love/hurt
                        me

        Who stole your heart?
        Maybe no one can say.
        One day you will find it,
        I pray.

Dawn is currently attending law school at the University of Baltimore, and affiliated with the lovely ladies of Sigma Gamma Rho Sorority, Inc. (EE-YYIPP). I don't consider myself a writer per se, I just put pen to paper when something troubles my soul.

Current words to live by, "Every man thinks that his burden is the heaviest", by Robert Nesta Marley.

==================================
Linval Hopeton London
==================================

ON THIS MORNING
(A wedding poem)

On this morning
I awoke
To the song
Of a bird
On the wing.
Its sweet song
Lilting softly
Through my window.

On this morning
I awoke
With the sun.
Its bright beams
Warming my
Skin,
Chasing the darkness
From my eyes.

On this morning
I prepared myself
For the day
Dressed in my
Best and
Hurried on my
Busy way.

LINVAL HOPETON LONDON - Linval, James to his friends, is 21, and currently living in Toronto, Canada.

" I started writing in early 1994 as a result of a broken heart, but it has become one of my life's greatest joys. My poems are mainly about love and the search for belonging, or trying to understand exactly what life is all about. I have a tremendous faith in God, and I thank Him greatly for allowing me to share my talents with all I meet. If it were not for Him, I would have crumbled long ago. With Him, I will always be strong."

On this morning
I walked through
The door
And left
Behind the
Lonely life
I once knew.

On this morning
I awoke
With love
In my heart,
Purpose in my soul,
And joy in my spirit.

For on this morning
I will say "I do"
To my companion,
To my best friend,
To my love,
For always.
My dear
I love you.

===================================
Linval Hopeton London
===================================

CRAVING

Are you satisfied
Knowing that
I can't get
You out of my
Mind?
Does it please
You to know
That my infatuation
Has become stronger
Deeper?
I now lay awake at
Night clutching
The sheets
In a desperate
Attempt to
Grab hold of
My fleeting love
For you.
On the edge
Of desire
I sit.
Perched as a hungry
Raven over
Its domain,
Of empty husks
And
Lonely fields,
At harvest's end.
Craving for a new day,
For a new beginning,
For a new love.

"The one thing that stands out in my life experiences is the strength I found when my parents separated. I have gained an insight into relationships that some people never will be able to see. I know the value of a soft touch in the morning, or a simple I love you before leaving for work. It can mean the world to some, and without it, life just ain't the same. So if there is one thing I've learned so far, it's that if you love, love with all your heart, soul, and mind, and never stop. God Bless."

```
=====================================
```
Marilyn Marshall
```
=====================================
```

MARILYN MARSHALL

Marilyn was born in Fort Sill, Oklahoma. She was in the Army, and travels quite a bit in the States and visits Barbados. She is a full-time wife who loves her husband, Anthony, and five children, Lydia, Rebecca, Belinda, Allen and Quintan. Marilyn's hobby is keeping Honeybees, and she plans to make candles that are made 100% out of honey.

MY SWEET KING, I AM ON MY THRONE

When you are not here, I worry about you.
The LOVE is so sweet,
I am on my throne that is YOURS to Keep.

My Doubts wander so throughout the Day.
Have you been with another, and you come to me here with your love to stay?
I greet you with a kiss, because our day has been long.

You given me many gifts, your Love is very Strong.
Whatever Doubts I have, is gone with the breeze.
KISS me with your chocolate lips, tell me whatever you Need...

I LOVE you and your heart is here to stay.
I am on my throne now,
Simplicity nothing can compare to or will sway.
Whatever that may be, will be with us.
We came too FAR to give up on TRUST.

My Sweet King, I am on my throne.
Join me and caress my Hand.
I have listened to you openly,
Let us stay with God's Plan.

When you are with me and I WITH you,
I see your Brown Eyes, so faithful and your aura is true.

Clean CUT relationship is what I needed.
I am glad to know you haven't cheated.

It is hard to keep a relationship pure.
There are so many obstacles to Endure.
I kept the faith and the Sun is so Bright.
You are on your throne, my Sweet King that
Keeps my heart through EVERY night.

=====================================
Marilyn Marshall
=====================================

Let me Take the Throne as your African Queen

Why have you been my giver?
You ask of me and I deliver.
You say you love me and I love you back.
You turn away from me time and time again to be an Overage Mack.
Stand Beside me African King.
Let me take the Throne as Your African Queen.

It seems like we are more Friends than lovers now.
We talk and we help each other out.
But there is so much truth we cannot face.
Never release your heart.
My past is tainted until YOU open my heart...
Now that my heart is open,
You went away.
I feel I need you so much but a part of you is never quite there
WITH Me.
I do not know where your heart belongs.
I just do not know.
All I can do is pray for you to be with me totally.

Why have you not been my giver?
You ask of me and I deliver
You love me and I love you back
You are turning away to be an Overage Mack.
STAND BESIDE me African King.

Let, ME
Take the Throne as your Wife and African Queen.

152

Silently I do not say too many words.
I know where you have been before and where you are.
Unconditionally, I love you always.
You are cherished by the many things you give me.
I admire your accomplishment.
The love we share brought US to a higher plain.
I rejoice in the fact I had your children to roam another generation.
Your heart is what I truly want to embrace.
If you just let it.
So all I can say is, "Stand Beside me African King."
Let me take the Throne as Your African Queen.

We are one, not many or several.
We share the same pain and tears and laughter.
It is so simple, if you just let it.
My love for you is true but will my heart ache if it is not the truth?
Why have you been my giver?
You ask of me and I deliver.
You love me and I love you back.
You turn away to be an Overage Mack.
Stand Beside me African King.
Let me take the Throne as Your African Queen.

Her faith in God is strong and unwavering. He has given her the strength to face challenges and live through extremely difficult situations. These life experiences taught Marilyn not to be judgmental of others, because you never know who can change your life.

"I really enjoy being a member of the Poets Niche. So much of the poetry, keeps my spirits up and inspires me in a lot of ways. "

===================================

Felicia Mason

===================================

360 Degrees

Sweet, Honey Dipped Chocolate,
Taste me In Your Mind.
Silky Smooth - Sleek - Golden Bronzed Skin,
Shimmering...Glistening.
My Aura Lights The Day - Illuminates The Night.
Truth Shines Through My Eyes...
My Loins Have Borne The Nations,
My Waters Sustaining All.
I Am Life.
Without Me -- There Is No Other.
All Men Seek the Shelter Of My Thighs...
See My Face, Hear My Voice --
Listen To The Rhythm Of My Heartbeat!
Know My Spirit, This Is Where You Live;
OVERSTAND
NUBIAN MAN, I AM LOVE.
And Like All Things, You Too Shall Return Home
For We Are One
And
Without You,
I Am
Not.

FELICIA MASON

Felicia was born on the South Side of Chicago, Illinois. She was in the United States Army for three years, traveled all over the United States, and lived in Germany for two years. Currently, Felicia is attending nursing school at the University of Alaska in Anchorage, but plans to move to Atlanta after graduation in December 1999. She pledged with the illustrious sisterhood — Delta Sigma Theta Sorority, Inc.

UNTITLED

One Day
While I was sitting
Listening for Whispers in the wind (minding mine)
You Called Me

Curiosity and Longing
For a Touch...
A connection...
A Black Man Who Beckoned My Answer...
I silenced my Wounds
And Covered My Mind's Eye
To The Lucid Deception
That is YOU

Cat-Like Movements
Body Of A God
Sun Dipped In Black...
You're All 'o That...
All 'o That!

And The Way That You Love Me...

I Melt Into Your Lips Like Butter
And Drip From Your Fingertips Like Honey
...With My Tears
And My Heart
That In Time ... You Will Break

I Know Because-
Because...
I can Feel Your Shadows
Surround Me

Still
I Want To Give You ... A Chance
I Want To Believe In YOU Black Man

But How...
But Still!
But How and Still...
You're Gaming My Feelings And My Friendship
And Somebody Else's Too ...I Think They Call Her Your Wife
All This is -- Is a F--king Game to You

I Want To Believe
(but why me)
I Need To Believe
(and why Now)
But I Know

I Gotta Let You Go...
I Gotta Let You Go!
Again

"My most notable contribution to humanity is my almost perfect son Neko, and helping sisters who need counseling. "

She is dedicated to this cause and chose the career of a Psychiatric Nurse Practitioner.

"My favorite atmospheres in life are Sunshine, Moonlight, Fresh Cleansing Breezes, Free Spirits and True Hearts."

====================================
Nicole McLean
====================================

NICOLE MCLEAN

Nicole grew up in Maryland, just outside of Washington, DC. As an only child, Nicole was blessed with a vivid imagination and a gift for story-telling. Over the years, she learned to use her talent in a way that allowed her to express her varied emotions in a positive and constructive manner.

Loneliness

Loneliness...
it fills my mind
invades my thoughts
overtakes my better judgment

how long will I feel this emptiness
how long will this pain last
how far does this vast expanse of nothingness stretch
how long will I doubt myself

God help me understand
your creation: myself

I
need
your
help

Help me to understand why
I feel deserted
alone
forgotten

I am afraid
...is this what loneliness is?

In the times You call me to be silent and sit before You
...those times when I don't obey Your voice
is this what lies there?

Pain
emptiness
nothingness
solitude
...that feels like solitary confinement
memories of things gone wrong
things I can't fix
imaginings of this emptiness stretching on toward forever...

well....
I don't like it!

Bring me the noise,
the clattering,
chattering,
irritating,
incessant,
unending sounds.
The bumping,
gyrating,
shaking,
vibrating,
reverberating,
sounds,
colors,
rhythms,
and smells of life being lived...
and experienced...
and tasted...
and enjoyed...

I'm not happy with the quiet
it scares me
it makes me
feel
so small
and inadequate

Oh!
I get it

this is where Your love steps in

well,
HURRY LORD

fix it
fix me
make me whole
before the loneliness kills me....
.....I am afraid
that I won't make it
if I don't figure out the puzzle
I'm certain
something terrible will happen

why do I feel that the fate of the world is in my hands?

...this is why I like the noise
the noise makes me numb
the noise drowns out the overflow of emotions

God
I have so much love to give
and nowhere to give it
and
when I sit still

it overtakes me
it shakes me
it moves me
it makes me ache inside

I tremble
it feels like an earthquake
in the pit of my being

Without an outlet
the tremors
shake me and
move me to
tears

but in the noise
I don't feel this way
in the noise

I only feel that life is being lived
all around me
and I'm learning
to understand
the noise
and find my place in it

God,
I'm so afraid...
what do You want from me?
The loneliness is killing me...
please...bring back the noise.

======================================
Nicole McLean
======================================

Damn...I'm almost 30!

I mean,
I feel HUNGRY all the time
I crave nourishment constantly
I eat until I'm full but it doesn't satisfy
I fill my home with the aroma of sweet smells
But it's not enough
It's as though all of my senses once deprived,
Have suddenly awakened and want to be used fully

My nose craves and searches for satisfying scents
You know
Like the smell of your man right as he comes out of the shower,
While he's still wet
All squeaky clean and manly at the same time
Or when you and your baby have just finished loving each other 'til you're
sweaty
And the sex funk mixes with the passion fruit oil and the vanilla candles
And you're so full and content you could just float away
Or how 'bout the smell of Sunday dinner just out of the oven?
Then you understand what my nose seeks

So
Can you understand then
Why my fingers and hands long to feel someone's skin
Especially when he knows how to care for his skin and it's smooth like a baby's
ass
And begs for your tongue and lips to trace delicate designs as intricate as mendhi
Or the feel of satin sheets against your silk negligee
How 'bout the heat from Grandma's fried fish right out of the pan?
You know
You could never wait 'til it cooled properly to pick it up for that first bite
Don't you get high siddity wit' me an act like you ain't neva ate wichyo hands
befo'...
I know better

While we're speaking on food...
How 'bout the taste of that secret spot that makes him wiggle...
EVERY TIME
You know that taste of power you have at that precise moment
When he's just a bundle of nerves...
Just worming and squirming around uncontrollably...
In YOUR bed?
Nothing tastes as good as that
Oh and let me give you a secret of mine
It's better with mango.

Ok... so I've got your attention
Well, my ears are craving excitement too
How else can you explain my wanting to hear
Roy Ayers and Busta Rhymes
Lauryn Hill and Rare Essence
Chuck Brown and DMX
LLCoolJ and Maxwell
Sade and Al Green
Jon B and Jimi Hendrix
All at the same time?

I love the sound of my name on his lips
Nobody can say it quite the way he can
And I never cease to be amazed
When I've got him tongue-tied and all he can manage is a moan

I know it's got to be medical attention I need
Because even my eyes are playing tricks on me...
I see him when he's not there
And you best believe that I see him everywhere

My vision needs stimulation
I crave loud colors and busy patterns
Red and orange
Blue and green
Stripes and polka dots
It really doesn't matter
I walk down the street and people appear to be multicolored.

Yesterday
I saw a lilac Latina with a blue bambino
This morning
An apricot colored African American diva said hello on the subway...
Hmph...my mailman is mauve most days
And lately,
My Kentucky-bred, blue-blood boss has been colored in kente and mud cloth
What's up with that?
Boy, I know his momma would scream to see him the way I do

When I wake up in the morning
I look blue
But after a vanilla shower
I feel like Venus through and through

I will say this about turning 30
I'm getting ready for one hell of a ride
And I can't wait to see what 40 has in store for me.

An aspiring entertainment attorney, Nicole is humorous, generous, feisty, spiritual and an exceptional friend to those that know her. She tells a great joke and makes a FANTASTIC cheesecake from scratch!

```
==========================================
```
Robin Porter
```
==========================================
```

No More Me

To love you for eternity
    is to love you till there's no more me.
To give you all I have and own
    to do the things that make you moan.
To share all of me high and low,
    to love you always - wherever you go.
To want the best for you in everything you do
    to just tell you again how much I love you.
To let you go when my heart says no
    to let you search for what you already know.
And when time is gone you'll know it was me
    for I will always love you - even past eternity.
Till there's no more me.

ROBIN PORTER -

Robin is from Houston, Texas. When she was younger, writing became one of her favorite hobbies.

"No matter how often I write, there is nothing like having someone identify or be touched by my words. If our eyes are the windows to our souls, then having the ability to write is having the privilege to share a little more of yourself with others....."

```
==========================================
```
Robin Porter
```
==========================================
```

A Rose

A rose

It's beauty;
So great
So powerful

So you.

Blooming.

Slowly,
Willingly,
one petal after
another.

Opening.

It's soul,

It's heart,
It's meaning to the world.

So you.

It's touch.

So Soft,
So gentle,
so unique.

So you.

Days Pass....

The Rose.

Wilting,
Falling,
Turning away souls.

The Rose.
You.
Days Pass....

You.

You are the rose.

Gentle,
Unique,
Soft,
Unseemingly beautiful,
Great,
&
Powerful.

You are me.

Me,
but only within you
Am I the .

".....My ultimate thanks goes out to the Lord and Savior Jesus Christ, not only for the ability to write, but the chance to experience those things that inspire me to write. I thank Him and love Him."

==
Karen Roberts
==

THE BOX

another box
just been carved
another mother
wiping tears
one more sista
left to pull up the rear

children growing up
without a dad
too young
to face
life can be so sad

no more three R's
we give them three C's
crack, cocaine and chronic
gave them a new language
called ebonics
got people running past the real problems
having histrionics

you're probably
wondering what i'm going on about
us killing each other off
gives the Klan more and more clout
they no longer need those sheets
cause my brothers are
shooting it out in the streets

KAREN ROBERTS

Karen is the proud mother of Tyrell and Kaylin. She is a Case Manager for the Department of Social Services. She was the leader of two Girl Scout Troops at the Roosevelt PAL, Brownie Troop 1044 and Junior Troop 1302. She is an active member of Church Of God In Christ, Little Zion.

Peace & Blessing,

Karen Robert

the hunt is on
and the prey is you
what's a sista to do
how can i make you understand
taking a life
don't make you a man

how do we stop it
takes more than
just say no
we must all stand up
or the killing won't go

reclaim your hood
your life
your head
or your kid
could be the next one
lying down in the street
shot dead

"I write about my feelings and how the world around me affects my daily existence. I wrote The Box after Tupac's murder. This poem was written for all of our young brothers who are gone too quickly."

=====================================

Karen Roberts

=====================================

Ready

I believe I am ready
to try this love thing again
I think I may have the answer
of what I need for my heart to sing

I believe I am ready
to give my heart anew
think it has more to do with me
than it has to do with you

I now know what I want
figured out what I won't take
don't have time for excuses
or love that comes too late

I've done some growing
on myself I did some work
that's why no more
little boys or even stupid jerks

Don't need to play the game
and no need to dumb down
maybe that's why I always ended
up with the out of work clown

See now I am a woman
and complete that's what I am
So now I know that I am
worthy of a real man...........

"I love my church family, and just would like to thank them for all of their love, support and prayers. I would also like to acknowledge DaQuan a/k/a Alonza Hopkins Jr., the man whom I love and will spend the rest of my life loving. I thank you for loving me to my core. You are my quiet in a world full of thunder!"

```
==================================
```
ANGELA GENEZ SINGLETARY
```
==================================
```

ANGELA
SINGLETARY

*Angela is a native of
Jacksonville, Florida, but
currently calls Atlanta,
Georgia home.*

*"I've been writing
seriously for the past five
years and my poems and
freelance articles have
been published by local
magazines and
newspapers in Atlanta
and Florida. My main
inspiration is life itself.
Whatever I'm
experiencing or seeing
through the eyes of
someone else literally
comes to life on paper. "*

revolution conversation piece

it's
gotta be
a little bigger than just you and me
outside appearances
or individual strategies
see we're dying out there
and just maybe you don't care
cause it's not directly affecting you
or
your world revolves around
whether or not
i look black enough
or if my words are
deep
dope
or big enough
but little boys know how to break down
a compound
of cocaine
rob
steal
and kill
as if they've gone insane
and what once was a world filled with
pink houses
baby dolls
and lipsticks
is now our reality of
babies having babies

cheap tricks
and little girls who think that having a man
is the sh..
revolution you say
i'm hearing every word
yet
i can't seem to focus on the situation
see my people are dying
 and we don't even cause a commotion
don't give a damn
or
just don't have time
for those emotions

===================================

ANGELA GENEZ SINGLETARY

===================================

are you in love with me

do i love you
now baby that's the easiest question
thrown my way today
i mean did marcus love africa
did malcolm love freedom
did zora love
love
now baby that's got to be the easiest question
thrown my way today
baby we are love
like
billie and her blues
you got me singing love songs
dancing
in the nude
loving me loving you
doing those things

169

that only you my love can do
do i love you
are the skies blue
and does the rain that touches you
touch me too
now baby that's got to be the easiest question
thrown my way today
did miles love those notes
that his trumpet
loved to play
did ella sing
what her heart was dying
to say
love damn sure ain't love
'til you give it away
do i love you
now baby that's got to be the easiest question
thrown my way
today
cause if this ain't love
then damn
ain't nothing left for me to say

"My claim to fame has to be the many influences of my artistic parents who taught me the beauty of art, specifically literature. I am currently working on my first novel entitled, No Guarantees."

```
================================
```
Sidney Singleton
```
================================
```

NO PRAYER GOES UNANSWERED

No prayer goes unanswered
when spoken earnestly.
For God's tender mercy
is for all eternity.

A heart that has been broken
is easy to offend.
And a spirit that is shattered
does not easily mend.

Rivers that are raging
flow into the sea
No man is an island
though some try to be.

There are reasons for tear drops
and reasons for pain,
In our weakest moments
there is strength we may gain.

So toil if you must
for just a little longer
The pains of today
tomorrow
will make you stronger.

No prayer goes unanswered
when spoken earnestly.
For God's tender mercy
is for all eternity.

SIDNEY SINGLETON

Sidney grew up in New Orleans, Louisiana, but currently resides in California. He attended Southern University in New Orleans, earned a B. S. Degree in Accounting, and is a tax consultant. He and his wife formed a poetry and song ministry called Comfort, Edify & Exhort (CEE). They have ministered in poetry and song at rehab centers, schools and churches throughout California.

==

Sidney Singleton

==

BLACK ORCHID

Come close my friend and have no fear
the spirit of love lingers near.
You my friend have weathered the storm
may the love in this poem keep you safe and warm.

In your lonely, lonely hours, love will be there
to caress your broken heart in times of great despair
The meditation of my spirit heard your humble cries
and put a song in my heart to kiss the tears from your eyes.

No mountain is too high for love to ascend
in time my sister, your broken heart will mend.
You are a melody that transcends time and space
you are the tears of affection on a young lover's face

You are a diamond, fragmented and blue
Oh precious one, it is love that touches you.
Love's spirit knows your suffering, love's spirit knows your pain
Love's spirit speaks the language that lovers understand.

Love endures heart aches, and love endures sorrow
love is the light of affection that will guide you tomorrow.
Love is something that you cannot possess
Love is sharing, and caring, its caring at its best.

Before I leave you I just want to let you know
that love will follow you everywhere you go.
And whenever you are down and feeling blue
just a little touch of love will surely see you through..

Because GOD is LOVE and he is much much more.

I LOVE YOU!

Sidney's message is timeless and his performance is dynamic. His contemporaries have dubbed him the Love Poet. However, he considers himself a Minister of Poetry. Sidney is currently working on a book of poetry and writing songs for a gospel CD.

==================================

Demeterius Smith

==================================

DEMETERIUS
SMITH - Demeterius' pen
name is FLITE. He is a
sophomore at Clemson
University, where he is
majoring in business
management. He is the
President of the Clemson
University Gospel Choir.
He accepted his call into
the ministry in 1998 and
receives the greatest joy
when he sees another
soul give their life to
Christ.

WHEN LEAST EXPECTED

The groom stands at the alter
But his bride doesn't show

The light turns green but the
Man slumped behind the wheel can not make the truck go

The father of the newborn looks to
His wife and says, "Honey lets name him Will"
But she doesn't reply, she just lays still

The young doctor's heart stops in
The middle of a toast to his family's health

A little girl falls to the ground
As her bicycle rolls on by itself

Before taking a nap a college student
Prays that he will pass an upcoming test
He never makes it to class, never awakes from his rest

Cheerleaders scream as their team faces off
Against their rivals in a game of basketball
The star athlete goes up for a dunk
His head hits the rim, he falls

People waiting at the church, wonder why the body has yet to arrive
None of them know, that as of five minutes ago, the undertaker is no
longer alive

At a family cookout the children play baseball in the yard

173

The ball hits one of them a little to hard

The night of the prom the girl waits and waits
The next day she still hasn't heard from her date

At a restaurant a woman says she has to go powder her nose
Unaware to her boyfriend, her soul is gone before the bathroom
doors close

In vain, firemen rush to the scene, for the flames have been
Set by angels with orders to let the world burn

As promised, when least expected
Jesus Christ has returned

=====================================
Demeterius Smith
=====================================

IT ONLY TAKES ONE SIP

It started when I turned thirteen
I was a teenager and I felt I was grown
I got tired of listening to my parents
I had rules that were my very own
I felt like a prisoner in my parents'
House and I couldn't wait to get free
My friends were the only people who understood me
One day one of my friends had a beer
And offered me a drink
Now, the older kids have always said
If you wanted real fun, then drinking was the thing to do.

And a lot of my family drank beer
So I thought what they were saying had to be true
One of my other friends had said drinking was bad for you
But I drank some any way, "What could one sip lead to?"

By the time I was fifteen I was drinking everyday
I started cutting class, so I could put a cold one away

By now I was smoking weed and cigarettes

And they were starting to have bad effects

I was depressed a lot and always in a bad mood
I got into a lot of fights because of my attitude
I made the mistake of having sex a lot
I didn't care if the person was older or younger than me
I thought they loved me, because it kept me from feeling empty

My teachers were getting on my nerves
They never paid attention to anything I had to say
So I quit school, I wasn't learning anything anyway

I got money anyway possible, why should
I keep a job when I could
Sell drugs, have sex, or steal
I was a hard-core thug keeping it real

I had loud speakers, name-brand clothes, and expensive
sneakers

I started pulling out guns to scare people
I felt that no one was my equal

One night at a party my life came to an end, all because
I was drunk and trying to show how hard I was

This guy bumped into me
And my friends yelled, "Get him. Show him that you are a real G"

I pulled out my gun and shot into the air until it was empty
The guy pulled out a gun and shot at me
I fell to the ground crying
Because I knew I was dying

The people whom I thought were my best friends
Just left me there on the floor
And I realized it was no fun trying to be hard-core

Never again will I stay up watching TV
Never again can I go the movies

I will never go to the prom or graduate
I will never go out on another date

I will never hear music or eat ice cream
I will never fulfill my dreams

I will never see my family or real friends again
I wish I had gone back to my parents' house again

I will never again crack jokes on the lunch line
I will never again get to see the sun shine

When I was thirteen I asked myself what would happen
If I took one sip

Now at seventeen, I am dead

Look where one sip has led

He spends his time writing, listening to music, helping others, and enjoying life. He would like to send shout outs to God, his parents, his siblings (Katrina, Peter Jr., Genobia), and to everyone who is down with STUDIO 44!

Something to remember: "If true love was a tear drop, than an ocean would not even begin to describe the love that God has for each of us!"

====================================

Katherine Smith

====================================

KATHERINE A. SMITH

Katherine was born in New Orleans, Louisiana, but currently lives in Dallas, Texas. She is the founder of a non-profit organization, Minority Resource, Inc. MRI is an Online Business Resource Center website that helps minorities, women and small business entrepreneurs start or maintain a business.

Colored

I am blue
or red
Both due to the bruises of society
I am purple

I am green
Like grass they walk on me

I am yellow
and pink
Flushed of my natural color
As a result of disease
In the minds of the greedy
and the hateful

I am orange
You see me through sun rays
The light that gives me strength

I am brown
Black
Which variations of these two
make up my shade of color

I am of no color

For in many eyes
I do not exist

Oui

You, me
Yes
We

How we fit together
naturally

The strength of your muscled mass
caress the curves of my slenderness

Ooooh weee!
Oui
Yes

We are in sync
as my body cups
your shape as you sleep
and when I move
you follow suit forming one

We
Yes
Oui

Your size, build, make
compliments mine

How we match in mind
and body
We are soul mates

Yes
Oui

We

Katherine Smith

Emancipated Again

How many times must I be freed?
In this lifetime
In the existence of a dark skinned human?

I Celebrated life rich with customs, beliefs and traditions
I Fought those who stole me away from my life and loved ones
I Ran when I was hunted like a rabid wolf

I Celebrated declaration of objectivity
I Fought for menial living allowances
I Ran from evils that lurked under white sheets

I Celebrated rights by law and constitution of this land
I Fought for equality - to be seen as human - with heart and soul
I Ran from the fear of what I represented - strength, endurance,
pride, intelligence and royalty
Yet perceived as never good enough

I Celebrated knowledge and the ability to learn -
To be educated without visual or legal barriers

I Fought invisible demons - segregation, separatism,
supremacy and the devil himself

I Ran from the drugs and violence that adds salt to the wounds
of society and breaks my slumber

I Celebrate Life as an African-American - Rich with customs, beliefs
and traditions blended with the freedoms that America promises.

In English tongue I claim my existence to be seen, heard and free
to live as we continue to fight the destroyers of souls.

I Fight for peace and unity - Growth is inevitable in GOD's plan.
He has tended to the needs of this world.

I Run from the corruption, immoral, indecent displays of
everyday life that are embraced and accepted as

FREEDOM

==

Tasha Tavaras

==

The Hush

Sweetly resounding
melodies in the
early fall air
moving in ways
yet unknown
softly sprinkling
like late dew
fluidly, floating
on thin wisps
of song whispering
ballads to the stars
producing sweet tears
that flow like rivers
or cascading streams
silently upon the
night air.

TASHA TAVARAS

Tasha started journalizing thoughts and feelings at the age of 8. At 12, these thoughts and feelings started to take shape in the form of poetry. Since then, writing poetry has been her passion. Her first poem was published at the age of 15, in a National Library of Congress Anthology entitled, Between the Raindrops. Her poems have also been published in various literary newsletters. The Poets Niche was the first on-line website to publish Tasha's poem Jonesin.

```
=====================================
```
Tasha Tavaras
```
=====================================
```

#L

Like an apparition
U came into my life
2 leave again
leaving me 2
wonder if U
were really here.
U loved
me once
and left
quietly
leaving your
fingerprints
on my heart
and tear stains
on my face
my memory
of U has
started to fade
but the imprint
U left on
my soul
will serve as
a constant
reminder
of your
love.....

Tasha is working towards her BA in English, with an emphasis on creative writing, and plans to earn her Masters and Ph.D. in Literature. She is currently working on publishing her collection of poetry entitled, Soul's Desire.

182

===================================
David Weeks
===================================

YOU ARE MY BLACK WOMAN

You are My strength, My Black Woman.
Without You, weakness destroys My spirit.
Your natural divinity brings out the
Fullness of My being. Separated We are
Incomplete, united We are Gods and Goddesses.
I am Your Man, You are My Black Woman.

You are My Mother, My Black Woman.
Your presence is imperative for My existence
To be. Co-creator You are, and the wisest of
All teachers; I can only dream to be like You.
You were ordained by GOD to care for and
Nourish Me, that I may fulfill My destiny.
I am Your Son, You are My Black Woman.

You are My Sister, My Black Woman.
The most beautiful woman to Me.
The strongest of all beings, I bow in honor
To You. The sands of time have come and gone,
Yet You have stood that I may not fall.
Yet, with all Your strength and beauty, I must
Still stand to protect Your femininity.
I am Your Brother, You are My Black Woman.

You are My Black Woman,
The One that understands Me.
I lift You up on a mountain high,
For all the world to see who strengthens
Me.

DAVID WEEKS

David was born under the sun on the beautiful island of St. Croix, Virgin Islands.

"I am a strong, spiritual, and positive Black Man. I am proud to say that my way of life is strongly rooted in the Knowledge of GOD. The one word that I think best describes me is Beloved, which is the English translation of my Hebrew name, David. Right now my poetry, which I consider as a duty to write, is one of the most important activities in my life....."

===================================
David Weeks
===================================

STILL WATERS

I go to the Still Waters to listen;
And I hear the cry of My Ancestors
In the bottom of that dark ship.
They were saying, "Hold On!"

I go to the Still Waters to look;
And I see the suffering of My forefathers
For hundreds of years held as slaves.
I saw in Their eyes, "Hold On!"

I go to the Still Waters to touch;
And I feel the pain and torture
My People had to endure.
I felt the pounding of Their hearts, "Hold On!"

I go to the Still Waters to inhale;
And I smell the open sores
And Burnt skin of Afrikans.
I smell the sweat from Their bodies, "Hold On!"

At the Still Waters I get strength.
At the Still Waters I Know who I am.
At the Still Waters I am reminded,
No matter what the situation, always "Hold On!"

Your Story is rich,
You Are Rich
Your future will be rich

ANCIENT
'99

ONE MOMENT

If Only For One Moment
I Would Like For You To Be Mine
For Us To Belong To Each Other
To Take Your Hands In My Hands
Make Our Union Divine

I Want To Lie Next To You
To Feel Your Energy
And For You To Feel Mine
To Shiver In Ecstasy As We Touch
Experience The Pleasures
Of One Another

For One Moment In Time
I Would Like To Feel Your Body
Pressing Against Mine
To Hold You In My Arms
To Know And To Love
Everything About You

I Want To Make Love To You
Mentally, Spiritually, And Physically
To Experience All That Is You
For You To Experience All Of Me

If Only
For One Moment
In Time
I Would Like To Taste Your Sweetness
Your Black Sweetness
To Get High
High From The Smell
Of Your Black Aroma
Black Juices
The Taste Of Sweet Nectar
I Take A Sip Of You

You Take A Sip Of Me

Open Wide
Your Pearl Gates
Lower
Your Golden Bridge
Let Me Enter Your Heaven
You Can Sit On My Throne
And Feel The Power
Of My Golden Scepter
You Can Rule My Kingdom
Take Full Control
Feel The Warmth
Of My Liquid Essence
Feel My Joy
Feel My Spirit

Oh Yes
For Just One Moment
In Time
Let Us Satisfy
Our Primal Needs
On A Higher Level
Let Us Share
With Each Other
The Sacredness
Of Making Love

"God has blessed
me with such a gift, and
to not use it, not share it,
not develop it, and not to
publish it to the world,
would be to turn my back
on God, to my people,
and to the world. I would
like to Thank GOD for
giving me life, for the
days ahead, and for
blessing me with the gift
of creativity."

==================================
Tamshi Williams
==================================

TAMSHI WILLIAMS

Tamshi was born in Spokane, Washington. Her parents were in the Air Force, which makes her an Air Force brat. Her family now lives in Cleveland, Ohio.

FATHER WHO

Who is my father: father who? Don't
know him to be; but he has set me free.

Are his eyes brown and hair Black? Would
he want to see me or just go back?

Can you be my father, or don't you bother?

At least look at me face-to-face; then
tell me if you want a place.

I've gone this long without a real father;
but I did have someone who wanted to bother

I love you for helping me to be; but now
that we both know, we are set free.

If we decide to be in one another's life;
I pray that it will not cut like a knife.

Father, Father, Father Who? I hope you
want to know me too...

===================================

Tamshi Williams

===================================

BLACK BY NATURE; PROUD BY CHOICE

God has blessed us with the darker pigmentation;
making others be filled with a jealous infatuation.

Our dark skin protects us from so many illnesses;
as well as provides an inner strength that God fulfills in us.

Society has tried to teach us that our history and
pride don't count for much; that's why it's so
important to bring unity amongst all of us and such.

We need to stand by one another in good and hard times;
pulling together all our nickels and dimes.

The pride in who we are and to whom we were born to
keeps our souls pure; followed by the intelligence
and spirituality that also makes us so sure.

There are some of us who choose not to have pride in
the skin we were born in; and those are the ones
that are committing the greatest sin.

We are the true Mothers and Fathers living on this
earth in a rut; when actually the majority should be
the squirrel trying to get a nut.

We own major companies in entertainment, publishing,
clothing, education and art; which as we all know
takes a whole lot of soul and heart.

Self awareness and self love; fits the Black Soul
like a glove.

Black by Nature: All the while fighting legislature;
Proud by Choice: As we all must listen to the
Motherland's voice.

We must inspire one another as the person inspired
this poem in me; coming as ONE people is the only
way to be set FREE.

Tamshi's major is Social Work and she is currently a graduate student. She works at a residential treatment center.

"I have always loved to write and enter poetry

MONICA BLACHE

Monica a/k/a moni, is the driving force behind the Poets Niche. Instead of a formal title, she prefers to be called "The Really Nice Person Who Keeps Things Running Smoothly at the Poets Niche." She also takes her roles as a loving mother, daughter, sister and friend very seriously. It's been said that "Once you've met moni, your life will never be the same."

==

Moni's poems

==

Holding the Silence and Held the Silence are based on how MEN and WOMEN see things and handle situations TOTALLY DIFFERENT. Sometimes, women jump to conclusions before giving a brother a chance to explain. Andddd, sometimes men take tooooo long to explain.

HERE'S HER VERSION AND HOW SHE SAW THINGS!!

HOLDING THE SILENCE

Silence has a way of holding you captive,
waiting for sound to break through

waiting for hope to make an appearance.

Silence has a way of bringing out character.

So when I said, "I Love You," and seconds
ticked away and silence entered the room

and moments claimed time and silence took
a seat to listen for a reply

and breathing stopped and silence also
held its breath

And, as silence squeezed its way in
between the space we just shared

I realized he hadn't replied.

I counted the words again.

3

So I said, "Did you hear me?"

His body language indicated he did.

Silence again slyly echoed its answer.

Silence somehow managed to contort the
face that just smiled down at me

drain the color out of the lips that
just kissed mine

twist the arms that just held me close.

Nothing was left to say because silence
claimed the truth as loud as thunder.

We just laid there holding the silence;

that deafening, unmistakable air of

nothing

****

NOW, HIS VERSION and how he handled the situation.

HELD THE SILENCE

I watched her face as she said she loved me.

Her skipping heartbeat counted the seconds I was speechless.
I sensed my silence made her feel sorry she loved me.

She turned away.

I hadn't held my breath out of fear.
I held the silence because I wish I'd said it first.

Those three words now filled my once empty heart.

I slipped out of bed and walked over to where she had turned away.

On bended knee, I took her hand and pressed it to my heart. I pulled her face
close to mine to breathe her air and said,

Understand and know this;
You are the reason I smile.
You are the answer to all my questions.
And, You are the very essence of why I love.

Underneath the pillow on which she laid, I pulled out a tiny blue velvet box

watched love sparkle in her eyes

and

held the silence.

=====================================
Moni's poems
=====================================

EASE

He always deceived with ease. He eased into his lies like a
comfortable pair of slippers. His breath never choked as the
words rolled out.

His canvas -- a woman's soul. His intent was to make his
victim swallow his deception with ease.

Everything about him was tailored, tasteful, orderly and never excessive. His timing was effortless, cool, calm and collected.

His aim was usually to please. He never coerced his prey into feeling weak. He simply eased you into believing he was doing you a favor by just being with you.

He used only essential words to make you believe he was interested, and left just enough vagueness to question your own sanity. Did he answer the question? Maybe. Did he say he'd call? Probably. Did he say he was coming over? We'll see.

He wanted nothing, and gave just that -- nothing. But somehow he convinced you he wanted more, simply by listening to your needs, or simply by nodding timely, or responding with I know what you mean, when you took a breath.

He was skillful not to share any part of himself. His past, fears and dreams, were all locked within this mosaic of a man.

As you may have already figured out, I was one of those unfortunate ones, a canvas, a victim, a silent believer in what was never there. A hoper of things he never shared. A pretender that he somehow cared.

You see, my self-worth was not based on how a man saw me in his eyes. I was educated, independent, and comfortable in my own skin.

I didn't need, or for that matter, want a commitment. I was content with the little things. A call whenever, dinner wherever or a trip no matter when.

I was sociable when the occasion called for it. Being a loner was a choice, not a sentence handed down by some man that I wasn't worthy of being loved. I just hadn't found Mr. Tolerable yet.

But it was at the end of the tenth year I wanted more. More than a call whenever, dinner wherever or a trip no matter when.

And, it was during a casual conversation with my father about my semi-reclusive lifestyle, I began to reflect on the ten years of nothing shared.

The simplicity of my father's comment that I was "Every married woman's nightmare," hit me like a ton of bricks.

And as I stood outside myself and watched stupidity unfold, "Every married woman's nightmare," rang in my ears and I swallowed my pride.

I'd never taken the time to ask all the obligatory questions or listen closely to the answers. His hypnotic voice and smooth mannerisms tricked my senses into believing whatever his answers were, were right.

And I rarely remembered hearing the sound of my name, Cassandra, cross his lips. It was always Honey, Darling, Sweetheart, when he phoned between 9 a.m. and 5 p.m., or Baby between 10 p.m. and 2 a.m.

His intentions were honorable, or so I thought. But actions do speak louder than words, and his actions were loud and clear.

"Every married woman's nightmare," was swirling in the pit of my stomach, and heartache was just about to scratch the surface of my sanity.

I'd never harbored any harm to anyone before. But all that changed when I followed him home in that 11th year and one day.

Dragging a child's bike, he eased out of his two-car garage. He kissed his lovely wife, who seemed as naive as me.

Later that night, he eased himself up from my bed, smiled, and said he'd call. I said, "Would you like a drink before you leave?" "Yes, Baby please," he replied with ease.

I watched him sip his drink as he dressed to leave. He never knew what hit him. "Honey, Baby, Sweethea---," he gasped as he looked at me with that ohhh sooo pathetic, panicked look.

> "So, how does it taste, Mr. Ease?"

The day this soulless ghost was laid to rest was the only time I went there. I stood out of sight behind a willow tree to feel the breeze.

I saw no headstone for a man who lived his life with such ease.
And as I left, I'm sorry to say, I was quite pleased.

I never thought of him until I received a note from Mrs. Ease, on the one-year anniversary of his sudden passing. I was stunned to receive this note, because I wondered how she knew about me.

Her note was instructions to his gravesite.

Four other women were there at the dearly departed's eternal home. And it was safe to assume they were also canvases, victims, and silent believers in what was never theirs.

His headstone was draped with an oversized picture of him he had apparently given to all of us. The one with the confident smile, innocent eyes, and premeditated heart.

And as we stood there silently paying homage to our pain, Mrs. Ease pulled back the drape and read the headstone with ease.

    That's What You Get For Being A Tease

=====================================
Moni's poems
=====================================

5 DAYS REMEMBERED

Spring cleaning.

It had been packed away for years in the left pocket of my brown coat. When I held it again, a tidal wave of emotions washed over me.

I fell to my knees and dusted off the box which carefully locked away the mementos of those five days we shared together.

There was nothing chance about our meeting. An improperly addressed thank you note to a friend found its way to his post office box. He sent it back with a note apologizing for opening it. He said he wished he had a friend like me who cared enough to send thank you notes. He said he liked the way I signed the note with a single letter - "m".

Now, scattered on the floor were seven hundred and forty-eight love letters he wrote to me for five years before we finally met, when the leaves turned red and orange.

He sent me a ticket, and the stub stamped "used" is what I held in my hand.
It's funny how time slips away, and another five years can separate people
for various reasons.
I closed my eyes and remembered.

I remembered the first sight of him.
I remembered his smile and thunderous laughter.

I remembered him holding my hand as we left the airport.
I remembered his first kiss melting away all of my apprehensions.

I remembered the beautifully wrapped heart-shaped wire basket
filled with new love letters written in calligraphy.

I remembered that the only sound that broke the silence was our
beating hearts.

I remembered slow dancing by candlelight.

I remembered the gentleness when he washed me in the fresh scent of
gardenias, and how he dried me in his homemade love.

I remembered crossing bridges of time and space, when we made love
under the sun and moon.

I remembered sleeping in his arms, and kissing him every moment of the day.

I remembered how I didn't want our time together to ever end.

I remembered with such the certainty that I'd never known before,
that I loved him.

I remembered the pain of leaving him and returning to my routine of details.

I remembered I couldn't understand why we weren't together anymore
after those five days.

That night, I slept on top of the seven hundred and forty-eight love letters
he wrote to me.

I put the ticket stub back in the left pocket of my brown coat, and packed
away those five days remembered until I needed it again.

Chapter Five

THERE'S NOTHING LIKE TEAM WORK!

INTRODUCTION

Teamwork is what the Poets Niche is all about. "David, I really love your poems, and I think we have similar writing styles. What do you think about us putting our heads together to write a joint poem and submit it to the group?" OR, "Saleem, that was deep. Have you noticed how we sign off on our emails? S&M? Sounds like a good poem to me! What say you?" OR, "Let's do a group poem for the book!" These are just samples of some of the conversations which may have taken place behind the scenes amongst poets who became admirers, then friends, and now collaborators.

===
Saleem Abdal-Khaaliq and Monica Blache
===

S&M

S was a man M knew from past lives.
Their paths crossed lifetime after lifetime.

It wasn't because they left things unfinished or
unresolved. It was because they promised to be
each other's light, fire, water, heaven and earth,
until death, which never seemed to happen.

Each time M took her first breath into another
century, a new frontier, or another galaxy,
S was always there to welcome her.

S was the author of M's life. She was the one
he wrote about in his search for unconditional
love. M was S's memory of each lifetime they
shared together. She revealed to him that life
itself was the lesson.

S was the only person who found the peephole
to M's dreams. M was the only person who made
it safe for S to dream with his eyes wide open.

For the S in he is the She in me
and the M in her is the Man I see
a whole divisible only unto ourselves.
Only M could give S back his flight
for this wingless bird had shaded his light.

While in the timeless Mind/Sense of it all,
each became mirrors to deflect their fall
Toward a coalescence -- their certain fate
For the S of SOUL and the M of MATE.

Our destiny was written in the stars, and our
footsteps marched to the beat of a different
drummer.

S knew M's history, and always whispered
the future in her ear. He shaped her thoughts
with just the sound of his voice.

M's laughter was a homing device which guided
S back to her arms.

And, their love was eternal because S is the Sun,
and M, the Moon!

The Solar passion of their love formed meteorites
of incredible intensity. A fusion of mind-thought.
The refraction of their very Being lifted the whole
of Humanity to Other Greater Worlds.

They became the songs, legends and mysteries
of the Universal Principle. A union remembered,
cherished and honored. A depth and density of
which no one could match. Their Light shone
beyond stars and was emulated and coveted by
those that knew its Glory.

S was sublime. M was Magnificent
Beyond this World, this Age, this Time
For M understood that

Seasons, and Shorelines bowed to her name.
Oceans and Rivers undulated under her glow.
Distance and Direction would be led by her
guiding Star.

He followed M into the Period of Time known
only as the Beyond Eternal. They had been there
before only to be returned to one another's arms.
Moving closer and faster toward fulfillment.

They stole time together, drank of the Neptunian
nectars of Joy, Harmony, Abundance and Peace.
Ate the Fruits of the Gods before them

and then...

M opened her eyes.

M felt the warmth of his arms wrapped around
her waist. S was snuggled behind her in a fetal
position.

S pulled M closer.

"Are you having the dream again?"

"Yes."

"Then welcome."

S kissed M.

The Sun and Moon

Eclipsed!

=====================================
David Weeks and /bams
=====================================

     duet
[one groove]

we come together
different voices
we know the lyric
different tune
we know the melody
different instruments
we know the harmony
different notes
we groove...

We understand The Music
The only TRUTH
We know The Truth
ONE MESSAGE
We know The Message
ONE RHYTHM

We know The Rhythm
ONE DANCE
Still We Groove...

you change the chord
i move in synch
you improvise
i recognize
harmonies blend
melodies soar
individual/intertwined
TRUTH sings out
TRUTH beats loud
one Jah/one God
one heart/one love
my drum beats
your soul speaks
we groove...

Yes
One Drum Beat
One Soul Speaks
You and I fade
Now it's just
I an I, ONE
One Voice
One Tune
One Instrument
One Note
One Groove!

==
Padmore Agbemabiese and L. K. "Rose" Ford
==

SO LONG THE ROAD

Like her mother, before her, she watches,
disdaining the wind, the sun, and the waves.
This soul at twenty is already sixty so much she has been through.
She speaks of others, from Angola to Guyana, Soweto to Nicaragua,
Brazil to India, Africa to America, and from Pretoria to Mozambique.

Standing alone through the cold, it's her voice alone,
with her song singing "It's me, It's me, It's me oh Lord,"
Standing in the need of prayer...

Hiding her tears in the ramparts of time,
Waiting to rest in the heart of a peaceful eventide.
She reads the pages of the daily news, Human life,
Destitution and Success.
Tall trees are hidden in the valley, it is into this scenery we walk.
It is only our spring dreams that whisper sadly,
It seems there is a breeze looking for the green grass in the valley
It's her voice alone with her song, "It's me, It's me oh Lord,"
Standing in the need of prayer...

Unable to sleep, she paces back and forth.
Separation hurts like "lifeless living"
She looked at the jeans he sent the kids
He has forgotten that she too lives.
Cutting the fleeting flowers in her garden
She is full of ancient heart songs.
Is there a dream to live on when years of
fullness are just stolen promises?
Looking at the tall trees, it's her voice alone singing,
"It's me, It's me, It's me, oh Lord,"
Standing in the need of prayer...

==
James London and Taheba Byrd
==

OUT TOO LATE

I am starting to get ready for our first date.
What dress will I wear to make you bring me near?
I have to make sure my hair is right so I will keep
you in my sight. Love of others have slowly dwindled
away as I await to start our very first date. I start
to think back to when we met, the romance in your eyes,
the emotions to me that were sent. The deep smell of your
cologne, the gentle arousing scent.

I am getting ready for the first date.
I wonder if I'll be good enough for you.
If I will be what you expected, what you want, what you need?
Did you say yes because you felt sorry for me
Or do I really stand a chance?
Tonight I'll find out.
Tonight will be my first chance to see what's inside you.
My first chance to view a bit of your soul.
To see if love is in your heart.
To see if I can make you mine.

I am also wondering what you are thinking and how would a
one-on-one be with you? If the words that come from your
tongue will be true. Will two hearts beat as one or will
they dance, souls untouched without any fun? Will I look
into your eyes and fall into your soul or will my thoughts
for you go untold? Will the door bell ring on time or will
you keep me waiting, and play with my mind?
Time will soon be here when you will come to me and
I will know if you truly care (you see)...
I have put on my armor to make sure my heart, which is made
of silver and gold, will be protected so my love for you
will not unfold...I know this is only a first date, a new start,
but I have to make sure all you are after is my heart!

I ring the bell and stand back from the door
At this moment I cannot do more.
I have prepared myself to sweep you off your feet
But all that is lost when your beautiful eyes I meet

You hair is done up to accentuate your eyes,
Your dress is a shimmering gown with a split up one thigh
Your beauty radiates like the moon in the night sky
The stars lose their brilliance as I look in your eyes
Your quiet beauty captivates me, your grace enchants my soul
But through all of the glitter, and through all of the gold
I long to see the part that you've hidden
The part I value, the part that cares
I want to see if in your heart I will find love there.

You enter the room, I am shaking within. Are you here for
my mind or out for my skin? The first hug was God sent me
on my way, made me feel good that you were with me today.
The look in your eyes, so soft, so gentle, so kind, so mild.
But back in my mind I am still living back in time when other
loves started off so great and then within the course of time
turned sour from the first to the last date...I will give it
a try. No, I will not get caught up in I'm your woman and you
are my man. I will try to take it slow and see how it goes...
And take the date as going out with a precious man and not have
the attitude that I know what I know...So show me what you came
here for, is it me that you want to endure? My mind, my soul is
an open door for those who had the key but don't claim it anymore...
but when you step out my door remember my mind is sharper than a
two-edged sword...Watch your words and make sure your hands you
claim, because a date with me is like riding on an endless train...
Make sure you bring your emotions, don't leave them out in the rain
.let's go...

So now we depart, we are on our way
To make history, to make a start, to begin anew.
We are blazing a trail through both of our souls
Will the trail stay clear or become overgrown?
Will we find at the end of our trek love or pain?
Will the fire of desire be doused by a bitter rain?
I don't know what will happen as we set out on our first date,
But I do know we need to hurry because we are running late!!
We need time to eat, and time to talk.
Time holding hands as we walk through a dark park.
Will you let me hold you close? Will you try to understand?
Will you look in my eyes and see I can be your man?
I long to know what secrets you hold in your mind,
What you hold in your heart, what you hold in your soul,

What will I find as we walk back to your door?

OK, we are in your car, a surprise place you are taking me is
it near or far. . .Driving along making small talk and I am
looking in your eyes thinking okay once again I am making a
brand new start. What will this night hold? Will you let me
go at my own pace taking it nice and slow? I find myself
falling within the small talk of your eyes, your cologne and
getting caught up in a danger zone...I know I have to
keep my cool and leave you distant and play by my own rules.
I can't take a chance of maybe jumping to any conclusions and
making myself feel like a fool. Your heart seems so tender, so
mellow, so kind. Are you the jewel I have been looking to find?
I roll down the window to feel the breeze trying to make myself
feel at ease. How will it begin or how will it end? Will I come
up with nothing but a pleasant friend or will the fire that comes
from the sun mend my heart with yours and make us one?

So now that we are on our way to the place we should be,
What are you thinking, what do you see?
Do you see as a man who could be more than a friend?
Do you see as a friend who's out for your skin?
Or do you see a heart that is faithful and true?
Who would rather tear down the sky
Than ever hurt you?
I don't know.
We drive on in silence, drive on through the rain
We pass a little park and I'm struck in the brain
Let's forget about the date, let's forget about the
formality of it all.
Let's just let our hearts guide us.
Let our spirits make the call.
So as I stop the car in the park on the way,
I only hope that this works out okay.
That my gamble will pay off, that you will see in me
someone to trust, someone to love, someone who cares
and would never let you fall.
Can you see this in my eyes as we sit on a bench in the park?

With the sun in the sky and warmth at my feet I sit on the
bench with the one so unique...My smile is so bright and your
tone is so pure...is it that you are the one I would like
to endure? The sweet smell of the humble summer breeze flows
through my hair and puts me at ease...When I look at you now

204

and think of you then, I would like to know what are you really
out for? Why a man so sweet so wonderful, so kind, so beautiful
.does he already have one or more? I wish right now I could
read your mind to let me know if I am wasting my time...The truth
that I would like to know is screaming from inside, watching you as
you smile at me. Is it only my body that you would like to glide?
Is it only a friend you need or are you trying to plant a new seed?
I look in your eyes and try to touch into your soul to try to figure
out what knowledge you hold...I know that I am ready now to begin
to start off slow and to be real friends...the needs I have for now
I will store and bring them out one by one to make sure that I will
stay safe and real and to make you know how I really feel...
I promise you I wouldn't rush you to be on a endless journey struggling
to break free...Look in my eyes and feel my warmth. Sit back and feel
my care within. Now you know you have a friend. Touch my smile with
your soul so my qualities won't go untold...and feel my cool gentle
style that you have not had in quite awhile!

THE GROUP POEM

A "GROUP POEM" was Saleem's idea. He wanted to do something
unique to see if all the poets could come together to write ONE POEM for the
book. After several conversations and numerous emails, here's what happened
and how "When Whirls Collide" was created:

/~~~~~~\

Date	:	Monday, October 26, 1998
From	:	Saleem Abdal-Khaaliq
To	:	Poets
Subject:		When Worlds Collide

IMPORTANT!!!! DO NOT POST YOUR RESPONSE TO THIS E-MAIL
TO ANY OF THE NICHES. Reply to moni only and here's why:

Let's show WALT our support and how he has INSPIRED US!

Your Mission: and I know you will accept it!

To Conceive, Formulate, Write, Create, Put Together and Come Up With --
One and only ONE: Collective -- Joint -- Together -- Collaborative POEM!
A death defying; signifying; I-Ain't-Lying; Round-the-World-Flying; kind
of thing! A "traveling poem," if you will, with the title of "WHEN WHIRLS

COLLIDE". In other words, to use your most creative, inventive and ingenious SELF to produce a single piece of poetry that we create that speaks of us and to US.

Each poet is to add one line (and 1 line ONLY) to the creation and pass it on to MONI ONLY. She in turn will pass it on to the next poet and so on and so forth. GOT IT?? BUT REMEMBER don't dally, because we are trying to complete this work by NOVEMBER 15th! 1998.

THE RULES:
(or as BAMS once said: "who made these ROOLES anyway?")

1. bams will start us off (Girl, can you write only ONE line? I know it's hard). bams will then forward her one line to MONI and ONLY MONI.

2. moni will be our relay person (in case one of you drops the ball, we won't tell on you but we'll know). That means once you have added your line to the piece immediately forward it on to ONLY MONI, and she'll see that it goes to the next poet.

3. moni will pass it via email ASAP and you need to do the same, reply to MONI, and ONLY MONI.

4. Remember only one line! (ONE LINE -- one line -- one ____).

5. Because time is of the essence, I ask that you do not discuss (via email or verbally) with anyone because not everyone has been selected to participate in this project. Also, no one (except moni) will ever know who wrote what line (except we'll all know that /bams will start us off).

6. ANY QUESTIONS? -- NO. Good let's begin!

But first, moni will need to hear from you if for some reason you won't be able to respond to your e-mails within the next week or so; because you're sick, tired, sick & tired, away, dead, your computer is broken, on vacation or whatever.

Thanking you in advance for your collaborative effort. SO LET THE GAMES BEGIN. ON YOUR MARK, GET READY, GOOOO!!!

Saleem

WHEN WHIRLS COLLIDE

(The Poets Niche Group Poem!)

...spinning quickly through the Depths of Time
and Memory, the Universe, in its infinite wisdom,
reached down and touched our Hand/Hearts.

All praises are due to the Omnipotent Creator.

One who possesses the Master Plan for eternal Love & Peace.
Love in the purest form. Our souls joined as One. For love has
no value, until given away.

So each of Us must express this love, through our own unique
righteousness. All of us must pass this love to everyone we touch.
Massage their souls in comfort and relief.

Let joy's welcomed entrance into our hearts and close the door, so it
won't leave.

As blossoms rekindle Spring, our Sun sunk deep, drowning all laments.
Through time the joy remains, from blessings well bestowed.
Like Moons, we all reflect from above a blue ribbon across golden sky.

Amid the horizon where we abide and the vision that is shared is when
our "whirls collide".

*Featured poets - bams, Mocha, Craig Gill, Rose Ford, David Weeks, Phaedra
Davis, Shawn Goins, Padmore, Eric Egerson, Linval London, and Saleem
Abdal-Khaaliq.*

Chapter Six

FEATURES

MONI'S TOP 10

To: Poets Niche 1; Poets Niche 2; Poets Niche 3
From: BlacheMD
Date: Mon, Jan 11, 1999
Subject: issue #14 - moni's top 10

* Nothing in life is accidental or coincidental *
moni (c) 1998

1) JUST A LITTLE HISTORY ON HOW & WHY MONI'S TOP 10 WAS
CREATED - In the beginning, POEMS OF THE WEEK was created to feature
our poets and spotlight their poems so all the world could enjoy. And, all was
fine in the Land of the Poets. Then, I started receiving fan email from members
about how much they were enjoying how I featured the poets by giving clues or
trivia questions. Members began emailing me birthday wishes, fun stuff about
themselves, websites to checkout, and prayer requests. So I said to myself, "Self,
why not share this fun stuff with your family so all can enjoy!!"

Recently, I randomly surveyed some of the members for their "HONEST FEED-
BACK" about moni's top 10. Here's what I asked: "I need your help. I'm trying
to get some feedback from members to see if they like the format I've been using
for moni's top 10. I'm not sure if everyone understands or even likes my dry
sense of humor. Please tell me what you think."

NOW, THE HONEST FEEDBACK I RECEIVED

From TW: I have to say that Moni's top 10 is very lengthy*no disrepect*. It has some good stuff in it, but some of it I don't get it. Not that I don't understand it, it's just that I wondering what does it have to do with poetry. I know you're trying to give the 411 on things, but make some of it pertain to poetry, K. You know I have much love and respect for ya.

From VeraCity: I happen to like the way that you have the top 10 set up. Sometimes, a sistah duzn't have the time to read through all of the thingeys, so every now and then I may peruse over the subtitles to see what interests me. And I kinda like your dry jokes!

From JL: I think your sense of humor is great....but that could be because I share it! I think the format is just fine....but a little more structure could help. Maybe a heading here or there, nothing major.

From AH: I saw the thing you put in your top ten about my birthday. . . (didn't quite know you were going to do that). boy was I surprised . . . but glad too!!

From DW: I really enjoyed Ur Top 10 this morning, it added to the positive feelings I have for 1999+....

From SH: hee hee. . . I have read your weekly newsletters. I think they are informative and your flow helps us in the niche feel as if we are family (as much as the web and our personal contact will allow, anyway). This is a pretty cool thing and no easy feat. No complaints here.

From AK: I love your format. It flows very well. It's like a summation of all the goings on both on the niche and in the community. It's cool the way it's formatted with areas of interest in the beginning and the poets of the week toward the end. That way it keeps everyone reading. Also, I love your poems at the end to sum up the week for the niche family. I say keep it just as it is.

To sum things up, moni's top 10 has now evolved into the Poets Niche Newsletter. I read through lots of miscellaneous stuff, as well as tons of email from our members, to keep everyone up-to-date on important events (birthdays, weddings, anniversaries, arrival of a new bundle of joy, job promotions, college updates, prayer requests, etc.) happening in the lives of our members. I hope I don't sound too preachy with some of the messages and try very hard not to offend any of our members.

I'm always keeping me eyes and ears open for helpful poetry hints. If you have any information you'd like to share with the group regarding poetry or non-poetry issues, please send it to me and I'll eventually post it.

---

2) MONI DOES IMPROMPTU RADIO INTERVIEW TO PROMOTE THE POETS NICHE - On January 5, 1999, I had my first radio interview on Q93 here in New Orleans. My so-called friend (CJ Morgan, New Orleans' top deejay) called me in between commercials and asked me to share with his audience information about the Poets Niche. With only 19 seconds to go, moni was on the air LIVE!!! (Somewhere between 16 seconds and 0, I lost consciousness). I tried REALLY, REALLY HARD not to embarrass y'all (although I did forget my name for a second until I heard CJ say it). His co-anchor, Monica Pierre (NOW Y'ALL KNOW I LIKEDDDD HER, cause of that Monica thang), chimed in and made me feel very comfortable. Those TWO MINUTES felt like a week. I must admit, however, I recovered quite nicely. So what happened next? I became an INFORMERCIAL QUEEN, telling folks how much fun we're having and how they can become a member of the Poets Niche.

From just two minutes of BABBLING, 14 people called to find out more about the Poets Niche. Of those 14 calls, 2 joined. SAY HELLO, if you haven't already, to poet and songwriter, Tina Marie Clark; and performance poet, Monique Nichole Fradieu. Monique will be performing on January 16th at the Community Bookstore (and I'll definitely be there checkin' my gurl out).

In the meantime, here's what Monica Pierre said: "You really expressed your vision well on Q 93 this week. I received a couple of calls from people very interested in what you are doing. . .Please give me a call to arrange an interview on my Sunday morning talk show, Quality Time with Monica Pierre.

If you want suggestions on how not to make a fool of yourself on the radio, while managing to increase membership, send for my book, "MY MAMA AIN'T RAISED NO FOOL, BUT MY DADDY DID!"

---

3) THE POETS NICHE BOOKSHELF - For the next quarter, we want to try something new to help our members prosper financially in the coming months. THE POETS NICHE BOOKSHELF will be a place for those of you who have already a published book (poetry or otherwise) to sale your books on-line. STAY TUNE for an email from Walt detailing how we plan to implement this experimental program.

4) COMING SOON!!! - If you have a website you'd like to link to the Poets Niche and we can link to your website, please email me with your URL address. Your website does not have to be a poetry link. It can also be non-poetry related - e.g., business, marketing, legal, how-to, etc. Networking is an important link to creating prosperity for our members.

---

5) MILESTONE - To date the we have received more than 540+ poems. The member who has submitted the most poems is: DRUM ROLL PLEASE !!!

Rose "bambam" Cooper - with 103 poems

FIND OUT NEXT WEEK HOW SHE DID IT and HER PLANS FOR THE FUTURE?

---

6) CONQUERING YOUR FEARS - Last year was a year of many "First" opportunities for me. First time using the internet. First time meeting and chatting on-line. First time hosting an on-line poetry group. And, the first time stepping outside of myself in 40 years to explore what makes me tick. I found out facing my fears head-on means less TEARS and more POWER. Whenever you feel apprehensive about tackling new challenges, starting or ending a relationship, beginning or ending an employment situation, relocating to a new city, sharing your feelings with someone without being mean-spirited, take lots of deep breaths, pray and accept prayers, then CONQUER YOUR FEARS!

much love
moni

To: Poets Niche 1; Poets Niche 2; Poets Niche 3
From: moni
Date: Mon, Feb 15, 1999 11:35 AM
Subject: issue #19 - moni's top 10 minus 2

HAPPY DAY AFTER VALENTINE'S DAY

(L) listening (O) openly (V) validates (E) everyone
moni (c) 1999

---

1) THE POETS NICHE GETS A FACE-LIFT, and Walt explains why -

moni: Why did you redesign the face of the Poets Niche?

walt: As one of the most popular niches within nichemarket.com, I've been
wanting to do something special for a while, but simply have been distracted by
other company stuff. The whole website is always changing. Much of what
exists now I'm sure will look different 6 months from now as we evolve. I
wanted the Poets Niche to have a look that reflected the growth, all of our
offerings and the "people power" behind the site's appeal and popularity.

moni: I'm sure you looked at many different websites to get some ideas. How
did you finally decide that this design, along with the graphics, would work best
for the Poets Niche?

walt: As I surf the net I'm usually on the lookout for two things: (1) new
"technology"; and (2) cool graphics. The collage of images (actual members of
the niche, by the way) is something I put together to complement the new
technology I found. For anyone who's into site design, the current format uses a
Javascript "mouseover" feature that allows the user to see more of what we offer
by simply positioning their mouse over the different "departments". The depart-
ment sub-headings pop up on the other side of the screen so the user doesn't have
to go too deeply into the site and get lost.

moni: Is it more user friendly?

walt: I think so, but that's for the members and visitors to let me know. I know the membership in the Poets Niche is up, and we're about to create a fourth group!

moni: And finally, how does the Poets Niche new look differ from the other websites on the internet?

walt: Hmmm. . .well, if I may be so bold as to rephrase your question, the "look" I'm sure is similar to sites out there. What sets us apart is what's going on "inside"! I wanted the reorganization of the content and the visitor's access to it to start to mirror the very interesting, special group of people who belong to the Poets Niche. I wanted the site to begin to tap into and reflect the amazing things that are going on behind the scenes, in the emails, on the phone, in face to face meetings; the fact that we're changing lives in a real way.

If you haven't already done so, Walt and I invite you to see the POETS NICHE NEW LOOK!! Please let us know what you think. By the way, as you surf the site, if you find any errors, blank pages, or get any errors, please let me or moni know right away.

I would like to personally thank Walt for the countless hours he devoted to redesigning the Poets Niche Website. Our motto is, The vision of one is the dreams of many. I'm grateful for Walt's visionary insight. For without his vision, many of us would still be sleepwalking. THANK YOU MY FRIEND!!!

---

2) GREETING COMMITTEE - Because of our increasing popularity, and new members joining everyday, we are now forming a Greeting Committee. Instead of everyone being notified when a new member joins the Poets Niche, the WELCOME WAGON will help our new members feel right at home. Anyone wishing to be on the GREETING COMMITTEE, please email me immediately at moni@nichemarket.com. And to our NEW MEMBERS, WELCOME ABOARD!!!

---

3) COMMENTS FROM THE PEANUT GALLERY - The Poets Niche "Peanut Gallery" was conceived as a way for poets and poetry critics to discuss the poetry submitted to the Poets Niche, beyond just saying "that was good" or "I liked it". With the understanding that criticism can and should be considered A Good Thing-- constructive criticism can lead to growth and insight, from both the artist and the critic. The aim of the Peanut Gallery is to provide a place for in-depth discussion of selected works, including commentary by the writer on

what the piece being discussed is about, if they so choose. Honest, thought-provoking opinions from peers is expected, and will be "webified" and kept on the Poets Niche webpage (www.nichemarket.com). Something to keep in mind: They Who Criticize About Spelling, Should Be Careful To Spel Rite Themselves. Some basic rules for the Peanut Gallery:

A) Once a week (depending on feedback), the moderator will select a poem to be discussed, and will contact the poet for permission in advance, giving the poet the option to send their own commentary to the moderator if they so choose. If the poets wishes to remain anonymous, please let me know when submitting your poem.

B) The moderator will then re-post the poem in its original form, along with any commentary from the poet, and invite members to send their commentary DIRECTLY TO THE MODERATOR ONLY at (bams@nichemarket.com).

C) Members who want to participate in the discussion will send their comments and critiques DIRECTLY TO THE MODERATOR ONLY at (bams@nichemarket.com), who will collect them through the announced period (the moderator reserves the option to follow-up on a comment to the critic). Also, if the critic wishes to remain anonymous, please let me know when submitting your comment.

D) At the end of the announced period, the comments will be condensed and posted on the Comments From The Peanut Gallery webpage, as well as announced in the moni's top 10. (Similar to Poems of the Week).

E) As the page says, "Can you handle it? Sometimes it's praise. Sometimes it's criticism. Sometimes it's suggestions...but always with love!". The Outside World will be cold and cruel enough when they start reading and criticizing our published pieces; we don't have to be cold, or cruel, in the Peanut Gallery. Just honest--and thick-skinned enough to take it when it's our turn. Remember: those who can't take it, shouldn't dish it out.

To kick things off and put my money where my mouth is, as the moderator, I will be the first "sacrificial lamb" to be critiqued by interested members. Though I have no problem with "hearing" blatantly honest (even mean-spirited) commentary about my works, if it would make folks more comfortable, comments can be sent to moni for this first piece at (moni@nichemarket.com) instead.

If you have any suggestions regarding the rules before bams' PEANUTS ARE ROASTED next week, please let her know as soon as possible. Thanks bams!

4) THE MEANING OF LOVE - I asked a few members to define love. LOVE MEANS:

From Mocha - Love is a natural high! It's unconditional, supportive, fun and demonstrates patience above and beyond one's "last nerve".

From Rose - Hmmm, my definition of love? That's a hard one. However, if I had to give a 'quote' on the definition of love, it would be, "Love is: "Finding the 'Mirror image' of yourself, treasuring that person above all others, then loving them enough to let them go, if that's what they really need." But hey, that's just my opinion.

From Felicia - Love is undefinable. . .when you think you have it -- you probably have something else; when you've given up, that's when it finds you ready or not, for better or worse. Love is never what we think it should be, never what we think it is; as we look closer it changes, but in the end we are rearranged and love remains the same -- being what it was all along, perpetually undefined and real nonetheless.

From James - Okay. . .let me see. Love is the one true thing in this world, the only thing that will survive into the next one, and the one thing that everyone wants. It could be as innocent as a hug from your baby girl, or as passionate as an intimate, midnight encounter under the stars. We are love, God is love, Love is. . .love.

From Katherine - Love is a fully encompassing feeling that makes one want to melt into the one that they love -- becoming one in the true sense. It strips you of all concern for self and increase the need to give more, care more, be more, achieve more. Love recreates your world into a colorful, vibrant, sunshine filled existence.

From Tamshi - What love means to me? Strength of commitment from your partner (faithfulness, honesty, consideration of feelings), respect in one another's goals in life and definitely support for life decisions. I also think that sensitivity, inner beauty and sensuality are key factors for me in the love game.

From Valentino - Love means looking past the imperfections of our minds eyes. . .and let your souls fly free amongst the clouds in the sky."

From Jaci - When there is no pain; when there is no hatred; when there is no fear; when there is no jealousy; when there is no pretense; when there is no camouflage. . .when all the sadness and falsehood and rhetoric have been peeled and stripped away. . .the tiny electrified core that remains is Love.

From Ajani - Love is the moment in time when everything you have ever wanted and worked for with every ounce of your being means absolutely nothing if compared to the perfection of a touch, a smile, an embrace, or an long antici- pated kiss made real. It's the moment when looking at your new born child, or one not so new, brings tears to your eyes at the humbling thought that you were blessed to be part of the process of bringing life. Love is a moment that doesn't have to last forever, but in it's simple slice of perfection, you'll always know it was there.

ANDDDDDDDDD FROM SUSAN HARRIGAN!!!

A true inspiration

Love means
peace of mind
peace in heart
to be true to oneself
and overcome the fear of the
person within

Love means finding the spirit of life
and love through and in
as many things you can experience
with your new eyes of hope

My faith has shown me love
My lover lets me live it.

No wonder there's so much love at the Poets Niche!!

much love
moni

==

EXCERPTS FROM A CONVERSATION BETWEEN MONI & SHENITA:

shenita said: I have often wondered how I could contribute to the Poet Niche's.
So many people write such wonderful poems. . .I used to write poetry, years ago,
but stopped. Unfortunately, I feel that I have lost the talent. However, I have
been blessed with the ability to inspire people through motivational writing. And
that's what I will contribute. I don't know when, I don't know how much, I just
know that it will come. . .I heard Les Brown speak this past Sunday and was "so
excited," I almost came into work to use the computer to write to the Poet Niche.
But, instead, I went home to savor the flavor of the moment. It was "oh so
good". . .I'm not quite sure where the Poet's Niche is heading but I'm so glad that
they picked me up along the way. God, it's so wonderful to be in the company of
progressive folks. . .If it's true that you attract people into your life who reflect
you, I must say. . .I must be projecting a wonderful image! Your efforts to unite
the family is incredible. Be blessed my sister. I'm so glad to be a part of your
family.

moni said: after eating 12 chocolate chip cookies & drinking a diet coke, i
sat down to re-read ur email in the privacy of my own home. . .you touched my
soul with such kind words. . .i'm delighted that u got 2 see Les Brown & i can't
wait 2 read ur motivational writing!! u'll never know what soul or heart u'll
touch or motivate with your words until U submit it. . .here's a thought! since
you feel "poetry" is not quite your forte, as part of moni's top 10 (either bi-
weekly or monthly), i can include a section called "FROM THE QUEEN'S
THRONE". . .this way, you can use this as a forum to use ur motivational writing
to uplift & inspire our members to continue reaching for the stars. . .let me know
what you think.

DRUM ROLL PLEASE! I PROUDLY PRESENT THE DEBUT OF

FROM THE QUEEN'S THRONE

Okay, I'm back.

Where have I been? In the bathroom crying. I just got off the telephone with
Moni, my beloved, and I started crying. I had to take a moment to thank God for
Moni, for allowing her to be used by Him, to assist me in my dreams and goals
of inspirational writing. God, you are so wonderful!
A friend of mine once told me, "You're never given a dream without the ability to

achieve it." As I grow older, wiser and closer in my relationship with God, I realize that this world will give me everything that I desire, if only I just believe. Imagine the possibilities! Imagine if you would just open your heart, again, to your childlike state. Remember when you used to dream of the possibilities? Remember when you use to think that you could do and be anything that you desired to do or be? But, somewhere down the road, you were hurt. Or, perhaps, fear set in, and then you thought to yourself that it would be easier not to dream. Easier not to hope. Easier not to aspire for the things that you truly desire.

Well, my friends, I'm here to testify that change starts from within. I'm here to tell you that God wants so much for you. The world belongs to Him. You are made in His image. All that He has, you have access to. Your life CAN be beautiful. Your life CAN be filled with joy, happiness, peace, prosperity, AND love. All at the same time! All you have to do is believe. All you have to do is aspire to align yourself to God's will for you.

I've decided to make a change. I'm giving my life to God and I thank Him for each moment because each second of the day allows me an opportunity to surrender all of me to Him. He is blessing me in so many ways. I am constantly watching my dreams and desires manifest themselves in my life. I am constantly in awe of God! I sometimes wonder what took me so long? I sometimes wonder why I hesitated? It doesn't really matter now. I'm at home and I promised God, I'll never leave! Won't you join me?

Be blessed!
==
FROM THE QUEEN'S THRONE by Shenita Vanish
February 15, 1999 - Issue #19 - moni's top 10
==

Did I tell you that I desire to be married, with children?

The interesting thing about life is that it will give you exactly what you desire. However, if your heart and your mind aren't in alignment, you'll cancel out your request. Often, we misjudge the cancellation and call the results disappointments.

Disappointment is when we say that we desire one thing but the result is something else. We expected one thing and received something else. I find that life is continually teaching me things that I need to know. I expect to meet a man that I will ascend into love with, get married and have children that will be spiritually enlightened. But how many times have I turned down an opportunity to meet a "nice" young man because I was (1) tired; (2) not in a good mood; (3) he was too tall; (4) he was too short; (5) he looked like he was one of those "know-it-all, advance degree brothers; (6) he lacked 'formal' education; (7) he was from the west coast - as opposed to the east coast; (8) he was from the north -- as opposed to the south, and the list could go on and on and on?

What do I expect? What do you expect? Do you desire a job that pays you $40,000 but say that you will accept a job that pays $25,000? Guess which job you'll probably get? Do you desire a mate who is financially secure and attentive but have been told that "if s/he makes money. . .s/he won't be able to be attentive. S/he'll be too busy working." So you give up one for the other?

If you align what you desire with what you expect, I am confident that God will provide for your every need(s) and desire(s). God hears our hearts. He speaks to our hearts. Let's not take the intellectual approach to life anymore. Let's listen to our hearts. Let's align our mind with our hearts/spirit and let God direct the way.

With this in mind, I am sure that God will not disappoint us. And with that in mind, look forward to my announcement, one day soon, of the delivery of the love of my life. Until then...continue to be blessed.

SHENITA VANISH

Shenita, self-named Queen, is a lover of life, a respecter of knowledge, a sincere romantic and a student of truth. The name Queen is in honor of her late aunt, Queen Vanish, who died in her teenage years and pays homage to her place in the world.

Given the talent of writing, speaking, listening, understanding and inspiring others, she is discovering her place in the world and finally understanding that to withhold her talents....

..... is to withhold God's blessing and grace to the world.

Born to a steady two parent, two-brother household and reared in eight cities and towns in the United States, Shenita is educated by life and three Historically Black Colleges and Universities. She is dedicated to uplifting those who have turned away from the light and believes in giving God the glory. It is in this manner that Shenita desires to bless the world with God-given talents.

219

AFTERWHIRL

The Poets Niche was created to quench the needs of aspiring poets searching for a place to share ideas with their fellow poets. Our quick rise to popularity was as a result of using the internet to spread the news that such a place existed. Recognizing the possibility that something unique could happen, we sprinkled hope, cultivated the minds, inspired souls, and the vortex effect pulled poets in from all over the country.

From June 1998 to January 1999, we received over 300 plus poems from poets eager to share their God-given talents with the world. The book you just read is from that enormous outpouring of love and infectious spirit of poets (or, as we lovingly call each other - Poets Niche Family Members).

COME INTO OUR WHIRL is a mosaic of gifted poets and a tapestry of souls, all united to articulate a common thread -- love of poetry and power of the written word. Writing poetry allows us to question our existence, explore options, resolve conflicts and express the human conditions we all face in search of satisfaction and love. Words have the ability to change minds, the power to console, express love, anger and despair, resurrect lost souls, and free one from their burdens. And, depending on how words are precisely arranged on the poet's canvas of plain white paper, words have the power to "move mountains".

Maneuvering through the minefields of the literary world can be tricky. Today's poets face a myriad of obstacles because poetry is not considered a marketable commodity. But, I guess they forgot to tell that to the great or up and coming poets such as Elizabeth Barrett Browning, Walt Whitman, Robert Frost, Carl Sandburg, John Ashberry, Paul Laurence Dunbar, Langston Hughes, Maya Angelou, Gwendolyn Brooks, Rita Dove, Nikki Giovanni, Jay Wright, Toni Blackman, Sonia Sanchez, or Kwane Alexander.

What to expect in the Year 2000? The members of the Poets Niche intend to dispel the myth regarding our worth as poets. In the Year 2000, and future years to come, our focus is to promote the work of aspiring poets and publish more books of poetry.

Walt's Friday Inspirations was the source which created the swirl, pulling thousands of hearts in which created this nationwide movement called the Poets Niche. We are now compelled to continue inspiring others to be the best that they can be, motivating souls to reach for the stars, and teaching mankind that happiness, wealth and love is an entitlement and is inscribed on everyone's birth certificate. We welcome you to stick around because our journey has just begun......

moni

Visit the Poets Niche at www.nichemarket.com

or

www.poetsniche.com

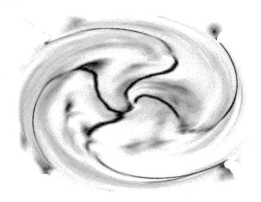